Explorations in Urban and Regional Dynamics

The task of modelling the evolution of cities – the dynamics – is one of the major challenges of the social sciences. This book presents mathematical and computer models of urban and regional dynamics and shows how advances in computer visualisation provide new insights. Models of non-linear systems in general have three characteristics: multiple equilibria, 'path dependence' over time and phase transitions – that is, abrupt change at critical parameter values. These phenomena all exhibit themselves in reality, and it is an ongoing task to match model-based analysis with real phenomena.

There are three key features of cities and regions to be represented in models: activities at a location – residence, health, education, work and shopping; flows between locations – spatial interaction; and the structures that carry these activities – buildings, transport and communications networks. Spatial interaction and many elements of activities' location can be modelled by statistical averaging procedures, which are related to Boltzmann's methods in statistical mechanics. This is while the evolution of structure can be represented in equations that connect to the Lotka-Volterra equations in ecology.

Within this broad framework, alternative approaches can be brought to bear. This book uses entropy-maximising versions of spatial interaction models. The authors explore the dynamics in more detail, using advanced visualisation techniques. These ideas have wide potential uses, and the book illustrates this with applications in history and archaeology.

Joel Dearden is a Research Officer in Computer Science at Swansea University, UK.

Alan Wilson is Professor of Urban and Regional Systems in the Centre for Advanced Spatial Analysis at University College London, UK.

T0347465

Routledge advances in regional economics, science and policy

Explorations in Urban and Regional Dynamics

A case study in complexity science

Joel Dearden and Alan Wilson

LONDON AND NEW YORK

First published 2015 by Routledge

2 Park Square, Milton Park, Abingdon, Oxfordshire OX14 4RN
52 Vanderbilt Avenue, New York, NY 10017

Routledge is an imprint of the Taylor & Francis Group, an informa business

First issued in paperback 2019

British Library Cataloguing in Publication Data
A catalogue record for this book is available from the British Library

Library of Congress Cataloging in Publication Data
Dearden, Joel.
  Explorations in urban and regional dynamics: a case study in
  complexity science/Joel Dearden, Alan Wilson.
  pages cm. – (Routledge advances in regional economics, science
  and policy)
  1. Cities and towns – Growth – Mathematical methods. 2. Cities
  and towns – Growth – Computer simulation. 3. Cities and towns –
  Mathematical methods. 4. Cities and towns – Computer simulation.
  I. Wilson, A. G. (Alan Geoffrey), 1939– II. Title.
  HT371.D43 2015
  307.76 – dc23
  2014040956

ISBN: 978-1-138-01914-0 (hbk)
ISBN: 978-0-367-86933-5 (pbk)

Typeset in Times New Roman
by Florence Production Ltd, Stoodleigh, Devon, UK

Contents

Figures

Tables

Acknowledgements

We are grateful to the following publishers for permission to use material.

John Wiley and Sons Ltd: 'A framework for exploring retail discontinuities', *Geographical Analysis*, 43: 172–87, 2011, used in part of Chapter 3; 'Using participatory computer simulation to explore the process of urban evolution', *Transactions in GIS*, 15: 273–89,2011, used in part of Chapter 7.

Springer Science and Business Media: 'Phase transitions and path dependence in urban evolution', *Journal of Geographical Systems*, 13: 1–16, 2011, used in part of Chapter 3; 'The relationship of entropy maximising and agent-based approaches', in *Agent-Based Models of Geographical Systems*, 707–20, 2011, used in part of Chapter 6; 'Tracking the evolution of regional DNA: the case of Chicago', in M. Clarke and J. C. H. Stillwell (eds), *Understanding population trends and processes*, 209–22, 2011, used in part of Chapter 8.

Anne-Sophie Bruno, *Histoire et Mésure*: 'Spatial interaction and structural models in historical analysis: some possibilities and an example', *Histoire et Mésure*, 2: 5–32, used in Chapter 8.

One of us (Joel Dearden) gratefully acknowledges EPSRC for a postgraduate scholarship.

We are grateful to Andy Bevan for Figure 7.3.

1 The BLV paradigm for urban and regional dynamics

1.1 Urban and regional systems and the BLV paradigm

The task of modelling the evolution of cities – the dynamics – is one of the major challenges of the social sciences. Cities are non-linear dynamical systems, and it is understood that models of such systems in general have three characteristics: multiple equilibria, 'path dependence' over time and phase transitions – that is, abrupt change at critical parameter values. These phenomena all exhibit themselves in reality, and it is an ongoing task to match model-based analysis with real phenomena. One real example was provided by the transition from 'corner shop' food retailing to supermarkets in the late 1950s and early 1960s (Wilson and Oulton, 1983). This was a very rapid transition almost certainly brought about by the crossing of a threshold associated with increasing incomes and car ownership, and therefore an ability to travel increasing distances.

There are three key features of cities and regions to be represented in models: activities at a location – residence, health, education, work, shopping and so on; flows between location – spatial interaction; and the structures that carry these activities – buildings, transport and communications networks. The main elements are shown in Figure 1.1.

It turns out that spatial interaction and many elements of activities' location can be modelled by statistical averaging procedures, which are related to Boltzmann's methods in statistical mechanics, while the evolution of structure can be represented in equations that connect to the Lotka-Volterra equations in ecology. The analogies are not exact, of course, and these methods have to be combined with others in the urban and regional context – for example, the account-based demographic and economic models – but the similarities are such that it is appropriate to characterise these modelling approaches to dynamics as BLV models: Boltzmann, Lotka and Volterra.

Within this broad framework, alternative approaches can be brought to bear. We use entropy-maximising versions of spatial interaction models, for example, though we could have easily used logit random utility methods, which are more or less equivalent. It is currently fashionable to use a framework of agent-based modelling or gaming models, and in later chapters we show how these approaches relate to our framework. We use the retail model to illustrate much of our argument, and we present the core analysis below and then explore the dynamics in

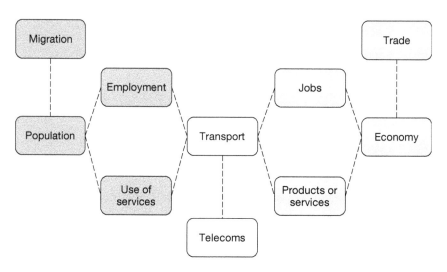

Figure 1.1 An urban system

more detail, using advanced visualisation techniques, in Chapters 2 and 3. We then extend the argument to examine the dynamics of a comprehensive model through a development of the Lowry model (Chapter 4). In Chapters 5 and 6, we return to the retail model and show how our analysis can be presented in agent-based and gaming forms. These ideas, of course, have wide potential uses, and we illustrate this in Chapter 7 with applications in history and archaeology.

The conventional retail model was first presented in its dynamic form by Harris and Wilson (1978). We build on this work – it is a useful archetype – and show how contemporary visualisation techniques provide a much deeper understanding of path dependence and phase transitions, and that this opens the possibility of making more direct connections than hitherto in identifying the effects of individual agents – in this specific instance, retail developers – in bringing about these transitions.

In Section 1.2, we introduce the retail model as our core example for use in much of the rest of the book. In Section 1.3, we build a demonstration model of the London retail system to illustrate the argument.

1.2 The core model

We proceed with a simple aggregated model to illustrate the ideas. Realistic disaggregation does not change the underlying argument. Define S_{ij} as the flow of spending power from residents of i to shops in j; let e_i be spending per head and P_i the population of i. W_j is a measure of the attractiveness of shops in j, which, for these illustrative purposes, we take as the logarithm of 'size' – reflecting range of choice and lower prices through scale economies. The vector $\{W_j\}$ can then be taken as a representation of urban structure – the configuration of W_js. If many

W_js are non-zero, then this represents a dispersed system. At the other extreme, if only one is non-zero, then that is a very centralised system. There is clearly, potentially, a measure of order in this specification of structure. The obvious 'order parameter' – a concept used in physics in relation to phase transitions – would be $N(W_j > 0)$, the number of centres that are non-zero. In a fully dispersed system, then, $N(W_j > 0)$ would be equal to the number of possible centres and would be large, while in a very centralised system, $N(W_j > 0)$ would be 1. We will see later that it is sometimes better to take $N(W_j > M)$ for some constant M greater than 0 as a better measure of structural change.

A spatial interaction model can be built by maximising an entropy function in the usual way (Wilson, 1967, 1970) to give:

$$S_{ij} = A_i e_i P_i W_j^\alpha \exp\left(-\beta c_{ij}\right) \tag{1.1}$$

where:

$$A_i = \frac{1}{\sum_k W_k^\alpha \exp\left(-\beta c_{ik}\right)} \tag{1.2}$$

to ensure that:

$$\sum_j S_{ij} = e_i P_i \tag{1.3}$$

and:

$$\sum_{ij} S_{ij} \log W_j = X \tag{1.4}$$

where $\log W_j$, as we noted earlier, is taken as the measure of consumer benefits and X an estimate of the total benefits achieved.

We also have:

$$\sum_{ij} S_{ij} c_{ij} = C \tag{1.5}$$

α and β are parameters (actually, the Lagrangian multipliers associated with Equations 1.4 and 1.5). Because the matrix is only constrained at the origin end, we can calculate the total flows into destinations as:

$$D_j = \sum_i S_{ij} = \sum_i \frac{e_i P_i W_j^\alpha \exp\left(-\beta c_{ij}\right)}{\sum_k W_k^\alpha \exp\left(-\beta c_{ik}\right)} \tag{1.6}$$

which shows how the spatial interaction model can be the basis of an activity location model since, in this case, D_j is a measure of retail activity at j.

Note that W_j^α can be written:

$$W_j^\alpha = \exp\left(\alpha \log W_j\right) \tag{1.7}$$

and the core equations can be written:

$$S_{ij} = A_i e_i P_i \exp \left(\alpha \log W_j - \beta c_{ij} \right) \tag{1.8}$$

where:

$$A_i = \frac{1}{\sum_k \exp \left(\alpha \log W_k - \beta c_{ik} \right)} \tag{1.9}$$

Thus, $\alpha \log W_k$ can be taken as a measure of the utility of an individual going to a shopping centre of size W_j but at a transport cost, or disutility, represented by $-\beta c_{ik}$.

A suitable hypothesis for representing the dynamics is (Harris and Wilson 1978):

$$\frac{dW_j}{dt} = \varepsilon \left(D_j - KW_j \right) \tag{1.10}$$

where K is a constant such that KW_j can be taken as the (notional) cost of running the shopping centre in j. This equation then says that if the centre is profitable, it grows; if not, it declines. The parameter ε determines the speed of response to these signals.

The equilibrium position is given by:

$$D_j = KW_j \tag{1.11}$$

which can be written out in full as:

$$\sum_i \frac{e_i P_i W_j^\alpha \exp \left(-\beta c_{ij} \right)}{\sum_k W_k^\alpha \exp \left(-\beta c_{ik} \right)} = KW_j \tag{1.12}$$

and these are clearly non-linear simultaneous equations in the $\{W_j\}$.

It is possible to characterise the kinds of configurations that can arise for different regions of α and β space: for larger α and lower β, there are a smaller number of larger centres, and vice versa (cf. Wilson 1981; Clarke and Wilson 1985; Clarke and Wilson 1986; Clarke *et al.* 1986; Lombardo 1986). This can be interpreted to an extent for a particular zone, say j, by fixing all the W_k, k not equal to j. The zonal interpretation is shown in Figure 1.2. The left- and right-hand sides of Equation 1.11 are plotted separately, and the intersections are the possible equilibrium points. If $\alpha \leq 1$, there is always such a point, but if $\alpha > 1$, there are three possible cases: only zero has an equilibrium; one additional non-zero stable state; and the limiting case the joins the two. The β value also determines the position of the equilibria. These graphs demonstrate multiple equilibria and path dependence. It also shows that as the parameters α and β (and indeed any other exogenous variables) change slowly, there is the possibility of a sudden change in a zone's state – phase transitions – from development being possible to development not being possible, or vice versa. These kinds of change are at a zonal level, but clearly they will trigger system-wide changes as well.

At this point, we can extend the analysis. In Figure 1.3, we plot initial values of W_j on the horizontal axis and equilibrium values on the vertical. When $\alpha < 1$, there is always a stable intersection between the cost and revenue lines. In this plot, there is a constant equilibrium size shown for all initial values (Figure 1.3a). For $\alpha = 1$, the gradient is finite at the origin (Figure 1.3b), so the existence of stable intersection depends on the value of the K parameter, which controls the gradient of the cost line. In the case shown, the equilibrium-size graph in Figure 1.3b shows a constant equilibrium size for all initial values and so is behaving like the $\alpha < 1$ case. For $\alpha > 1$, the gradient is zero at the origin (Figure 1.3c) and the revenue curve either intersects the cost line twice or not at all (excluding the

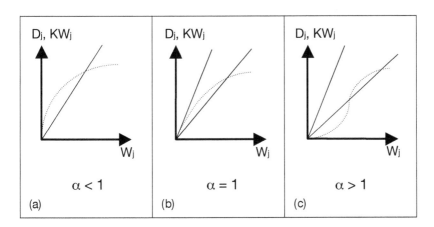

Figure 1.2 Revenue-cost curves for varying α

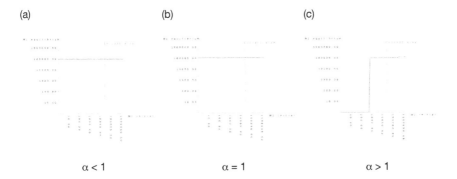

Figure 1.3 Initial value plots for varying α

origin), and so highlights the possibility of multiple solutions in the system. This is demonstrated in the equilibrium-size graph in Figure 1.3c, which shows that there is a critical initial value of W_j. Below this value, the centre is ultimately not profitable, and above it the centre grows.

What we know from the analysis of Figure 1.2 is that, at a zonal level, there are critical values of α and β, for example, beyond which only $W_j = 0$ is a stable solution for that zone. So we know that there are critical points at a zonal level at which, for example, there can be a jump from a finite W_j to a zero W_j, or vice versa). This implies there is a set of α and β at which there will be critical changes somewhere in the system. Here, there will be many more system phase transitions, but in each case consisting of a zonal transition (which then affects the system as a whole – since if a W_j jumps to zero, then other W_ks will jump upwards, or vice versa). It would be interesting to see whether the set of critical αs and βs form a continuous curve – and if we add 'K' as a parameter, then we would be looking for a critical, possibly continuous, surface.

This analysis shows that almost any change in model exogenous variables can, in principle, bring about a phase transition. For example, any change in the $\{e_i P_i\}$: then we are looking for a many-dimensional critical surface. We could possibly take the argument a stage further and build on the fact that equilibrium solutions in non-linear models are path dependent: we would expect to find phase transitions along some paths, but not on others for the same model with different initial conditions.

1.3 An example: retail centres in London

To illustrate the argument, we construct an aggregate demonstration retail model using London data. This is not intended to be realistic, but simply to show what is involved in the process of trying to find and interpret retail/urban phase transitions. The database is shown in Figure 1.4. It consists of 633 residential zones and 215 retail centres. (Retail data is from the Town Centres project, 2002, and population data is from the 2001 UK census.) The model represented by Equations 1.1, 1.2 and 1.6, in terms of flows and revenue attracted, and Equation 1.12 are solved for the equilibrium $\{W_j\}$. The methods are presented in detail in Dearden and Wilson (2008). The results of a model run are shown visually in Figures 1.5 and 1.6. Figure 1.7 shows a grid of (α, β) values with a model run for each element of the grid. One element, a model run displayed in 3D form, is shown in Figure 1.8.

1.4 The next steps

In the next two chapters, we explore more fully the range of possible phase changes and (in Chapter 3) the implications of these for planning – in particular, while the non-linearity of the models inhibits their use in long-term forecasting, whether model-based analysis could be used to avoid undesirable phase changes and to encourage desirable ones. A particular kind of transport investment that would be registered as $\{c_{ij}\}$ changes, for example, could bring about a desirable phase

Figure 1.4 The initial conditions for the London illustration

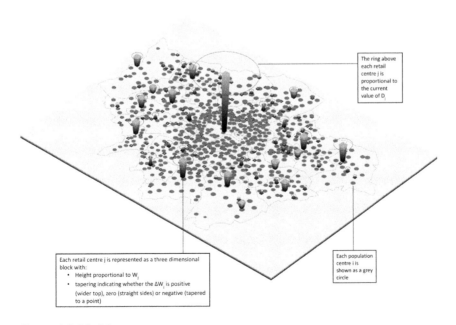

Figure 1.5 Model outputs

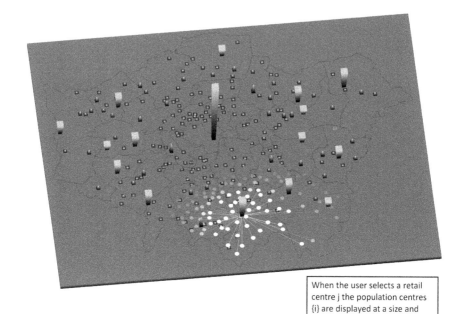

When the user selects a retail centre j the population centres {i} are displayed at a size and opacity proportional to S_{ij}

Figure 1.6 Model outputs showing flows

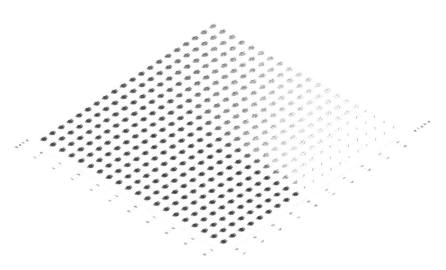

Figure 1.7 An (α, β) grid

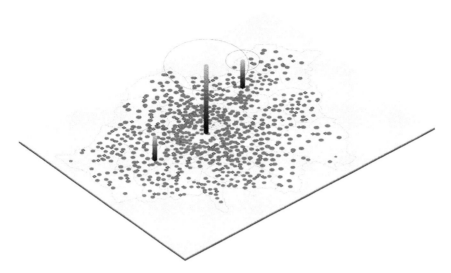

Figure 1.8 Retail centres for one run on the grid [$\alpha = 1.1$, $\beta = 0.20$, $\varepsilon = 0.0001$]

transition. More generally still, we will use a 'DNA' argument to explore the possibilities of transition given the structural starting point – a 'genetic medicine' approach. This takes the initial conditions of the structural variables as limiting the space of development possibilities. This is in itself valuable policy and planning information, but we could also pose the question: What should be changed in this structure to bring about a desired transition?

References

Clarke, G. P. and Wilson, A. G. (1986) *Combining Theoretical and Empirical Research in Retail Location Analysis*, Working Paper 468, School of Geography, University of Leeds.

Clarke, G. P., Clarke, M. and Wilson, A. G. (1986) 'Multiple bifurcation effects with a logistic attractiveness function in the supply side of a service system', *Systemi Urbani*, 7: 43–76.

Clarke, M. and Wilson, A. G. (1985) 'The dynamics of urban spatial structure: the progress of a research programme', *Transactions, Institute of British Geographers*, NS, 10: 427–51.

Dearden, J. and Wilson, A. G. (2008) *Exploring Urban Retail Phase Transitions – 1: An Analysis System*, Working Paper 140, Centre for Advanced Spatial Analysis, University College London.

Harris, B. and Wilson, A. G. (1978) 'Equilibrium values and dynamics of attractiveness terms in production-constrained spatial-interaction models', *Environment and Planning A*, 10: 371–88.

Lombardo, S. R (1986) 'New developments of a dynamic urban retail model with reference to consumers' mobility and costs for developers', in D. A. Griffith and

R. J. Haining (eds), *Transformations Through Space and Time*, Dordrecht: Martinus Nijhoff, pp. 192–208.

Wilson, A. G. (1967), 'A statistical theory of spatial distribution models', *Transportation Research*, 1: 253–69.

Wilson, A. G. (1970) *Entropy in Urban and Regional Modelling*, London: Pion.

Wilson, A. G. (1981) *Catastrophe Theory and Bifurcation: Applications to Urban and Regional Systems*, London: Croom Helm.

Wilson, A. G. and Oulton, M. J. (1983) 'The corner shop to supermarket transition in retailing: the beginnings of empirical evidence', *Environment and Planning A*, 15: 265–74.

2 Phase transitions and path dependence

2.1 Introduction

A wide variety of techniques are used to model discontinuities in urban evolution. Catastrophe theory (Thom 1975) provided impetus and was developed in the context of urban systems by Wilson (1981). Another approach using cellular automata (Batty 1998) and multi-agent systems (Bura *et al.* 1996) explores the emergence of self-organising structures from micro-level behaviours in systems existing far from equilibrium. Batty (2005) highlights the potential for discontinuities to occur in such systems and Dendrinos and Mullally (1981) uses dynamical systems theory to demonstrate how discontinuities can occur in the evolution of city-size patterns. Straussfogel (1991), applying Allen and Sanglier's (1981) model based on the theory of dissipative structures, outlines the difficulty of detecting bifurcations. Approaches based on fractals have a clear link to dynamical systems theory and can generate realistic urban forms (Batty and Longley 1994; Benguigui and Czamanski 2004). As far as we know, there is no standardised way of detecting discontinuities.

We focus on retailing to illustrate the argument. As we saw in Chapter 1, Harris and Wilson (1978) developed one of the first dynamic retail models that looked at discontinuous change within the system. This model was later applied at a finer scale and extended by Fotheringham and Knudsen (1986) to include locational rent, external scale economies and agglomeration of retail outlets. Similarly, Lombardo (1986) introduced a more detailed cost function and demand-side dynamics. These ideas have also been taken forward by a number of other authors; for example, Lombardo *et al.* (2004) connected these ideas to the agent-based modelling framework. Other explorations were offered by Clarke (1981), Clarke *et al.* (1986, 1998), Borgers *et al.* (1991), Nijkamp and Reggiani (1987, 1988), Oppenheim (1986), Phiri (1980), and Rijk and Vorst (1983a, 1983b). A different model, based on space-time differentials, was used by Baker (1994) to explore how trip frequency is affected by shopping centre size, and identified critical values at which large and small centre behaviour occurs. Part of the difficulty of understanding discontinuity in these approaches has been the complexity of the systems and models themselves. Here, we tackle this by using modern visualisation techniques to reveal the structure of the system and allow it to be explored in detail.

We use these ideas to build up a framework for identifying and analysing discontinuities in urban models.

The Harris and Wilson model, described in Chapter 1, is used as a simple archetype to illustrate the new framework. This can be developed in a straightforward way to incorporate further refinement. In Section 2.2, we explain our framework for detecting and analysing discontinuities. Section 2.3 shows the results of applying this methodology to two examples – the Greater London and South Yorkshire retail systems, which allows us to explore the policy applications for this technique. Some concluding comments are offered in Section 2.4.

2.2 A framework for exploring discontinuities

We first present the retail model of Chapter 1 in discrete time form to make our procedures explicit. Recall the basic definitions. S_{ij} is the flow of money from residents of zone i to shops in zone j; e_i is spending per head and P_i the residential population of zone i. The c_{ij} parameter represents the cost of travelling from residential zone i to retail zone j. W_j is a measure of the attractiveness of shops in j and in our illustrative model here we take this to be measured by floor space. The vector $\{W_j\}$ can be taken as a representation of urban structure. The difference equation form of the model can be represented as follows:

$$\Delta W_j\left(t,t+1\right) = \varepsilon\left[D_j(t) - KW_j(t)\right] \tag{2.1}$$

for the period $(t, t + 1)$. Then:

$$W_j\left(t+1\right) = W_j\left(t\right) + \Delta W_j\left(t, t+1\right) \tag{2.2}$$

The equilibrium position is given by:

$$D_j = KW_j \tag{2.3}$$

which can also be written out in full as:

$$\sum_i\left[\frac{e_i P_i W_j^\alpha \exp\left(-\beta c_{ij}\right)}{\sum_k W_k^\alpha \exp\left(-\beta c_{ik}\right)}\right] = KW_j \tag{2.4}$$

As we have noted, it is well known that for non-linear systems there is the possibility of multiple solutions; solutions are dependent on the initial conditions – 'path dependence'. There are discontinuities: that is, there are critical values of the parameters – such as α and β, but in fact any exogenous parameter or variable – at which the structure changes suddenly.

Equation 2.1 generates a path through time that will be highly dependent on the initial conditions. These conditions are unlikely to be near an equilibrium set, and if ε is relatively small, a timeline will be generated that may take a long time to reach equilibrium, but will in some sense be governed by the underlying equilibrium – the retail structure will tend towards that, however slowly. In practice, of course, other variables that are assumed to be exogenous and fixed will actually vary, and so to construct real timelines it is necessary to make some assumptions about these. In order to explore discontinuities, therefore, we first focus on equilibrium retail structures, $\{W_j^{equil}\}$. We therefore solve Equation 2.1 iteratively, not interpreting each iteration as a passage of time – simply as a mathematical device for finding the equilibrium solution to which, other things being constant, the system is tending. To make this plain, we use n to count iterations so that this is not confused with the elapse of time, t. Hence, we write Equation 2.1 as Equation 2.1a below:

$$\Delta W_j \left(n, n+1\right) = \varepsilon \left[D_j(n) - KW_j(n)\right] \tag{2.1a}$$

where n is now an iteration number. If we wish to construct a timeline that assumes that each time-step is from one equilibrium to another – because of a change in otherwise exogenous variables between t and $t + 1$ – then the solution at time t could be designated as $\{W_j^{equil}(t)\}$. We could then present the evolution of the system through time as the sequence:

$$\left[\left(W_j^{equil}(t)\right), \left(W_j^{equil}(t+1)\right), \left(W_j^{equil}(t+2)\right), \left(W_j^{equil}(t+3)\right), \ldots\right] \tag{2.1b}$$

The heart of the structural criticality problem is whether, at the location of a particular zone, j, conditions permit a non-zero value of W_j. If there are many such locations, then this will be a distributed retail system, and vice versa. A task for the framework, therefore, is to simulate that analysis. It is difficult to isolate what is happening in a particular retail zone because, as the equations show, each W_j equation shows a W_j dependence on $\{W_k\}$, $k \neq j$ (Wilson 1988). To make progress, we make the assumption that D_j can be plotted against W_j, assuming that all the $\{W_k\}$, $k \neq j$ are fixed. The equilibrium condition can be written:

$$D_j\left(W_j\right) = W_j^\alpha \sum_i \left[\frac{e_i P_i \exp\left(-\beta c_{ij}\right)}{\sum_{k \neq j} W_k^\alpha \exp\left(-\beta c_{ik}\right) + W_j^\alpha \exp\left(-\beta c_{ij}\right)}\right] \tag{2.5}$$

to show explicitly the dependence of D_j as a function of W_j, assuming all the other W_k are fixed.

It was shown analytically in Chapter 1 that there are three cases – shown in Figure 2.1, which is repeated here for convenience. The cost, KW_j, is also plotted and is, of course, a straight line. At equilibrium, the $D_j(W_j)$ curve and the KW_j line will intersect. In Figure 2.1a (in which $\alpha < 1$), the gradient of the $D_j(W_j)$ curve is infinite at the origin, and so there is always an intersection with the cost line, and that can be shown to be stable. Thus, for $\alpha < 1$, we would expect a dispersed system. In the Figure 2.1c case, $\alpha > 1$, the cost line either intersects the curve twice (excluding the origin) – as shown by the lower gradient straight line – or

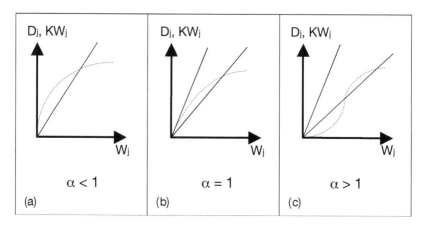

Figure 2.1 Three variations of the $D_j(W_j)$ curve

only at the origin – as shown by the other line. In the former case, the upper intersection is stable and a non-zero W_j is possible; in the latter case, W_j will be zero. More centralised patterns will have many such zeros. $\alpha = 1$ is a special case (Figure 2.1b). The D_j curve has a finite gradient at the origin and the possibilities of intersection generating a stable point are like the Figure 2.1c case. We should therefore always expect a discontinuity at $\alpha = 1$.

This analysis illustrates the possibility of multiple solutions to the equations: in the Figure 2.1c case, there are two possible solutions; if there are many zones in such a state, this indicates multiple solutions for the system as a whole. The particular solutions 'achieved' will depend critically on the initial conditions, and we need to specify these – starting values for the $\{W_j\}$ and the $\{e_iP_i\}$ – and, of course, such $\{W_j\}$ will not be equilibrium values. When (and indeed, if) the iterative process converges, Equation 2.3 will be satisfied. We iterate through the equations using a specified set of model parameters – essentially, solving Equation 2.1a. The parameter values and initial conditions determine whether a stable equilibrium can be found.

The retail systems we analyse here have large numbers of retail zones, which means we cannot visualise the phase trajectory of the system as we might with a system of two or three zones. Instead, we use a three-dimensional representation of the system, which visualises the position and floor space of each retail zone and then uses animation to convey the variation of the system variables as it iterates towards equilibrium or over time. We communicate the important quantities at each iteration using size, colour (if available) and shape. Retail zones are illustrated with three-dimensional blocks whose height and tapering indicate floor space $\{W_j\}$ and growth rate $\{\Delta W_j\}$, respectively. Each residential zone is shown as a circle on the map with a diameter proportional to its spending power (e_iP_i). The whole model is presented on top of a boundary shape file for our region of interest, which provides a sense of locality and helps us quickly identify the various parts of the

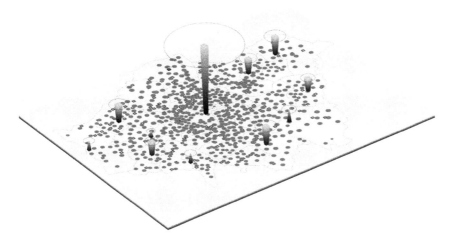

Figure 2.2 One iteration from a single-model run

system. There is also the option to visualise the money flows into any retail zone ($\sum_i S_{ij}$) and out of any residential zone ($\sum_j S_{ij}$) during a model run. Figure 2.2 shows the output for one iteration from an example model run. In order to retain the potential for a retail zone to be revived from zero size, we enforce a minimum retail zone size of 1 m^2.

We now present an algorithm for detecting discontinuous change in the aggregate retail model. We embed the equilibrium configurations, $\{W_j^{equil}\}$, of the system on a grid in some subset of the parameter space. First, we set the initial conditions of the system by initialising the $\{W_j\}$ and $\{e_i P_i\}$ using real or hypothetical data. We then choose between one and three model parameters to investigate for discontinuous change. For each one, we define a range and a step size to produce a set of discrete points. We have defined a one-, two- or three-dimensional model parameter space, which contains a number of unique parameter sets. For each of these, we run the model from our initial conditions to equilibrium and save the resulting $\{W_j^{equil}\}$. The grid then contains the equilibrium configurations of $\{W_j\}$ for the specified parameter ranges. We initially use α and β – and we can look for the presence of discontinuous change between neighbouring parameter sets. We can label two configurations as $\{W_j^P\}$ and $\{W_j^Q\}$ and then define a measure of difference θ between P and Q as the sum of the absolute difference across all retail zones:

$$\theta^{PQ} = \sum_j \left| W_j^P - W_j^Q \right| \tag{2.6}$$

The differences in $\{W_j\}$ configurations in parameter space can be visualised – in the 2D case – by taking α and β as X and Y coordinates and plotting θ as a

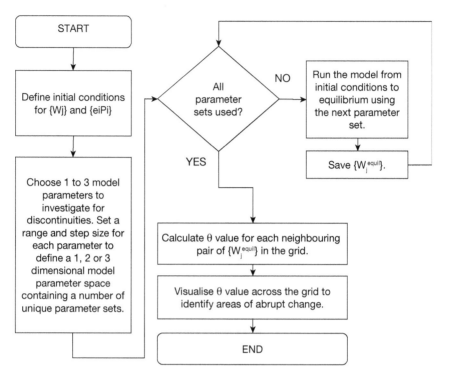

Figure 2.3 Algorithm for generating a results grid

boundary line between each pair of neighbouring configurations. The algorithm is summarised as a flow chart in Figure 2.3.

We use computer graphics to visualise a large amount of detail in the results grid, which allows us to move around and explore it. Each $\{W_j^{equil}\}$ in the model parameter space is presented in the same way as that shown for a single model run, allowing us to identify the size of individual retail zones. This technique uses the idea of dimension stacking (LeBlanc *et al.* 1990) to embed two geographic dimensions into one, two, or three dimensions representing the model parameter space. This is illustrated by the example results grid shown in Figure 2.4, which embeds the British National Grid Easting and Northing into an α, β parameter space. Feiner and Beshers (1990) introduced a similar system for displaying financial data. There is the potential in the future to take this further and visualise a larger number of dimensions recursively. We introduce the θ plot in the next section.

The results grid is illustrated for the Greater London retail system. The data sources are detailed in Appendix 2.2. We search a two-dimensional area of the (α, β) space in the range 0.1–2.0 using an 81 × 81 grid. Clarke and Wilson (1985) did a version of this analysis – but contemporary graphics generate a more powerful representation.

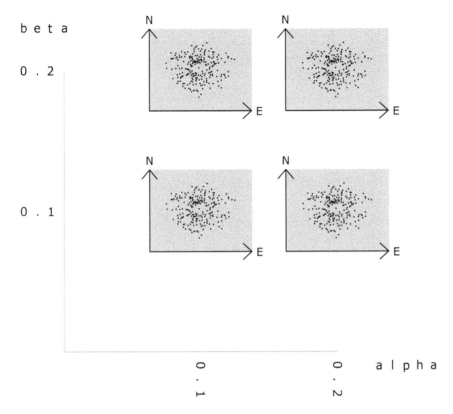

Figure 2.4 A two-dimensional results grid

A θ plot is shown in Figure 2.5. A large number of 'fault lines' can be seen running through the grid, each of which represents a discontinuous change in the system.[1] One of the most prominent fault lines at F represents the previously predicted discontinuity that occurs as $\alpha = 1$ is crossed. The advantage of visualising the θ plot and results grid in real time is that one can look at what is actually occurring at the level of individual retail zones. Crossing fault line E in Figure 2.5 leads to the appearance/disappearance of a smaller retail zone (Romford) near one large central retail zone (Central London). We can analyse this change by first selecting a pair of parameter sets, one on either side of the fault line (Figure 2.6), and second by plotting a D_j, KW_j zone graph for Romford for each parameter set. The graphs are from the fourth iteration of each model run because this is where the rate of change for this zone diverges between the different model runs. We can see in Figure 2.6a that there are two intersections, an unstable lower intersection and a stable upper intersection, whereas in Figure 2.6b the $D_j(W_j)$ curve does not intersect the KW_j line. The black dot on each graph shows the W_j value of the retail zone on the fourth iteration.

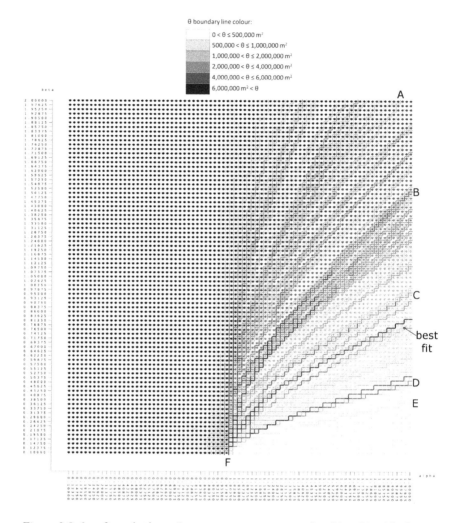

Figure 2.5 θ surface plot in α, β parameter space on top of an 81 × 81 grid of results

We calibrated the model by calculating an R-squared value for each $\{W_j^{equil}\}$ in the results grid compared to the initial $\{W_j\}$. Figure 2.7 colours the parameter space by the R-squared value of each parameter set. The best fit[2] $\{W_j^{equil}\}$ compared to the real data is at $\alpha = 1.95250$, $\beta = 0.78875$ with an R-squared of 0.78 (marked in Figure 2.5). In order to explore this in more detail, we generate another grid centred on the best-fit parameter set (Figure 2.8). The results grid covers the space defined by varying α from 1.934 to 1.970 and β over 0.770 to 0.806 (all to three decimal places). The ridges near the best fit in Figure 2.5 also run through Figure 2.8 and are easier to distinguish at this resolution. The position of the best

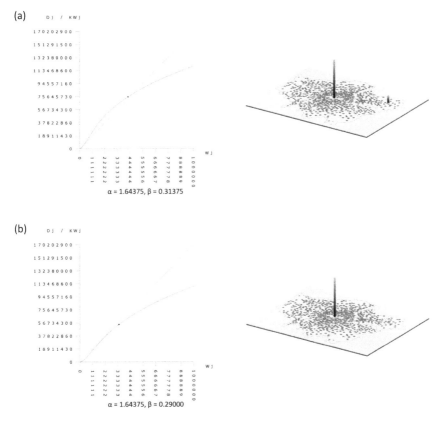

Figure 2.6 Zone graphs explaining the appearance of an edge city called Romford
(zone graph plotted after four iterations for parameter sets either side of
a ridge in parameter space)

fit suggests that a change in α or β could cause a discontinuity to occur in the system that would cause a shift in the position of one or more edge retail zones.

The results that appear in the grid above, and therefore also the discontinuities, are influenced by the initial conditions fed into the model. Starting with a different $\{W_j\}$ as our initial conditions would produce a different set of discontinuities. This suggests there is the potential to influence the behaviour of a retail system and, if desired, improve its stability through properly informed planning.

It is useful to pursue the London case in more detail, and, for illustrative purposes, we concentrate, as implied by the (α, β) grid in Figures 2.5 and 2.8, on phase transitions in (α, β) space. We consider a possible phase change along fault line D in Figure 2.5 where a two-zone system changes to a five-zone system. We identify two result maps, one on either side of the possible phase change, in Figure 2.9.

Harrow appears as an edge city when there is a decrease in α (the impact of retail zone size on consumer shopping destination choice). The initial versus

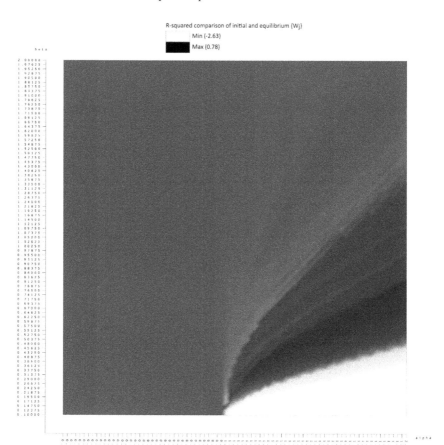

Figure 2.7 α, β parameter space coloured by R-squared comparison of each $\{W_j^{equil}\}$ in the results grid compared to the initial $\{W_j\}$

equilibrium size plot in Figure 2.9a shows that Harrow is not profitable for any initial size below about 143,000 m². With an initial size of 125,500 m², Harrow is not a viable centre in this configuration. In the initial versus equilibrium size plot Figure 2.9b, however, we can see that Harrow is profitable from 74,000 m² upwards. Harrow's initial size puts in inside this range and allows it to grow to a size shown by the flat plateau on the right-hand size of the graph. The height of this plateau is fairly constant across the range of initial conditions that reach it, though the exact value depends on the impact of the initial size on other zones. Exceeding this plateau size in the initial conditions will cause the zone to shrink back to the size of the plateau (indicated by the diagonal line). If the initial size of Harrow was less than 74,000 m², we would not see Harrow appear, showing the dependence of the system on initial conditions. Figure 2.10 shows equilibrium-size graphs for the other three centres that appear in the phase transition in Figure 2.9.

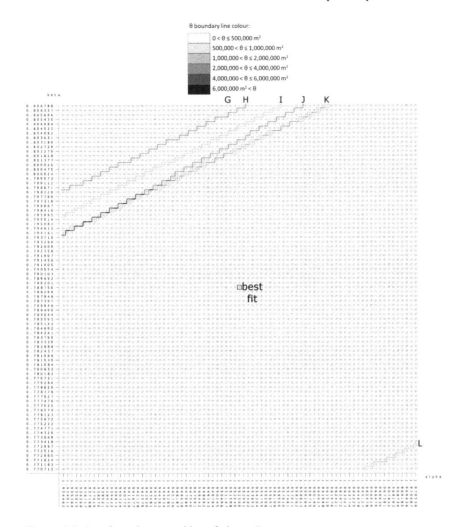

Figure 2.8 θ surface plot around best fit in α, β parameter space

All the graph pairs show a similar pattern to that of Harrow, supporting the idea that rapid changes in many zones simultaneously can bring about a phase transition.

These equilibrium-size graphs provide us with a critical size (W_j) below which a retail centre is not viable given the available spending power in the population nearby and the competing retail zones in the system. To demonstrate this idea, we can modify the initial size of the four edge retail zones that appear in the phase transition in Figure 2.9b. We set the size of each below its critical size. Figure 2.11 shows the resulting equilibrium state both before (Figure 2.11a) and after (Figure 2.11b) this modification to the initial conditions. The large central retail zone remains largely unchanged; however, the four old retail zones on the

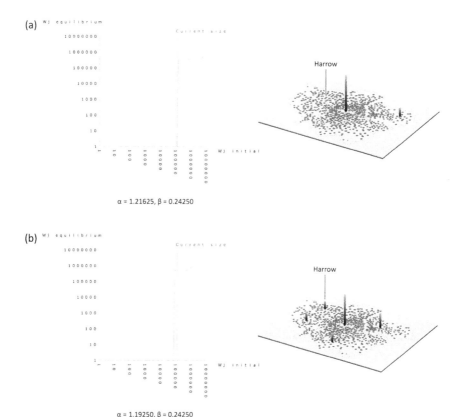

Figure 2.9 Structure either side of a phase transition with equilibrium-size zone graphs for Harrow; the change in Harrow's critical size accounts for its appearance/disappearance through the phase transition

periphery are replaced by three new retail zones: Southall, Bromley and Romford. It is interesting to note that the general shape of the retail system is preserved.

To help us understand the potential for change across a system, it may be helpful to look at all the retail centre critical sizes together. For this example, we have switched to another region, South Yorkshire, a metropolitan county about the same area as Greater London. The initial conditions are shown in Figure 2.12. The region has far fewer retail zones and so is easier to reason about for this purpose. Figure 2.13 shows how the critical size relates to the initial conditions size for each of the retail zones in the region. This was generated using the best-fit model parameters found above for Greater London. The aim here is to move towards providing a view on how interventions in a retail system may or may not be supported by self-organising processes (in this case, market forces). As with the Greater London model, the figure is only intended to be illustrative of the technique rather than a comment on the state of the retail system in South Yorkshire.

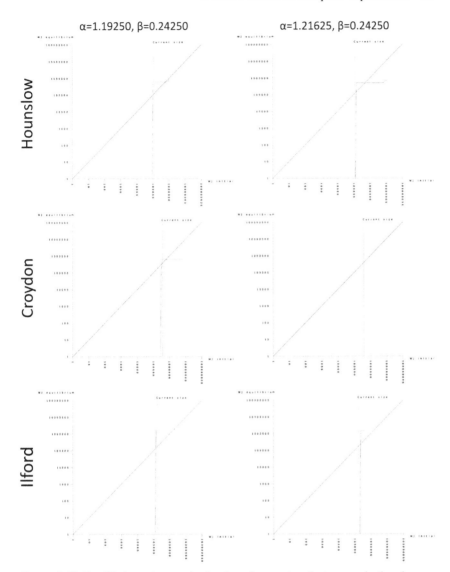

Figure 2.10 Equilibrium-size graphs for the other centres that appear in the phase transition

2.3 Using the analysis in planning contexts

We can use the insights gained from this analysis to demonstrate two potential new forms of analysis. First, in relating model predictions to reality, we can take account of agents, in this case retail developers, by showing how they change the 'initial conditions' at a point in time and possibly bring about phase transitions by their actions. In this way, it should be possible to give an account of the history

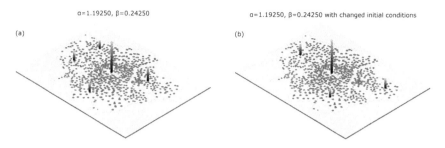

Figure 2.11 The results of changing the initial conditions informed by equilibrium-size graphs demonstrating path dependence

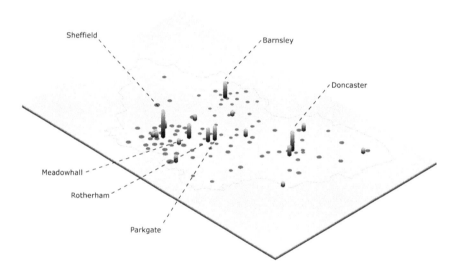

Figure 2.12 The South Yorkshire retail system

or urban development – in effect, as a sequence of initial conditions, illustrating path dependence. Second, the model could be deployed on behalf of a developer wanting to build a new shopping centre. The analysis tools described above could be used to calculate the size that the new centre would need to be in order to compete effectively in the current retail market: that is, the minimum size, as a new 'initial condition', to guarantee stability. In the same way, the analysis would provide a maximum size. In the rest of this chapter, we explore the second of these ideas in relation to South Yorkshire.

Rotherham is a major town in the area that featured in the news in 2009 because almost one-third of its high street shops had closed down (Addley 2009). This

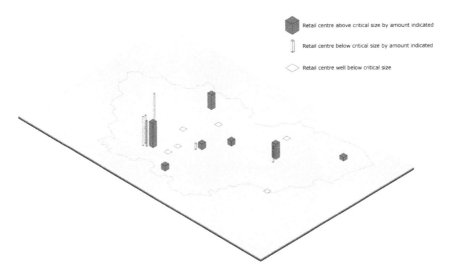

Figure 2.13 Critical size markers for all South Yorkshire retail centres

has been attributed to various factors, including recession and competition with two nearby out-of-town shopping centres: Meadowhall and Parkgate. The local council attempted to reverse the decline with various policies, including subsidising costs for new retailers and free parking after 3:00 p.m. At the time, the British Retail Consortium (Hunt and Slater 2009) highlighted the fact that town centre retailers across the UK were facing similar challenges. They advised that:

> Town centres are assets which need to be managed and we need to focus on centres which are already at, or approaching, 'tipping points' rather than waiting to tackle the much more difficult task of High Streets already in decline.

We can see from comparing Figures 2.12 and 2.13 that the critical size (~133,000 m²) for Rotherham in the 2004 data is about 25 per cent above its size in the initial conditions (~105,800 m²) – meaning that, in our model, it will decline without at least a further investment of about 27,000 m². The zone graphs for Rotherham either side of the discontinuity are identical on the initial iteration; however, by iteration 67, we can see major differences. The zone plot in Figure 2.14a for $W_{Rotherham}{}^{initial} = 105,800$ m² shows that the $D_j(W_j)$ curve never intersects the KW_j line at any point except the origin, so pushing Rotherham to zero, whereas the plot in Figure 2.14b for $W_{Rotherham}{}^{initial} = 134,000$ m² shows a stable intersection at about 115,000 m². This may point the way to a methodology to identify the point at which high streets 'fail', either in a recession or in competition with out-of-town centres.

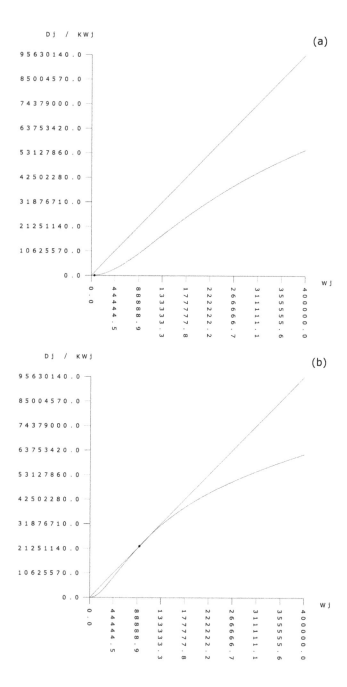

Figure 2.14 Zone graphs for Rotherham on iteration 67 of the best-fit model run with (a) $W_{Rotherham}^{initial} = 105{,}800 \text{ m}^2$ and (b) $W_{Rotherham}^{initial} = 134{,}000 \text{ m}^2$

2.4 Concluding comments

We have demonstrated a relatively simple and widely applicable software framework for identifying and analysing discontinuities in a simple urban retail model using semi-realistic data. The visualisation capability is an important part of the system, which allows discontinuities to be explored in detail. The technique has the potential to provide useful insights for decision-makers in both government and retail businesses in order to better understand the impact of planned changes to a system. For example, when commissioning new out-of-town shopping centres, one might look at the conditions required to create a reasonable balance of demand at both the high street and out-of-town shopping centres.

There are many avenues of further research to pursue. The cost function, KW_j, is a retail zone production function, and more realistic functions should be explored along with alternative rent functions. At the expense of considerable computing power, it should be possible to overcome the assumption that in constructing the zonal graphs, all (W_k), $k \neq j$, are fixed. In constructing the $D_j(W_j)$ curve, for each W_j point, the model could be rerun to equilibrium maintaining the condition of constant total floor space. Once the zonal graphs can be produced with greater accuracy, their properties can be explored as a set for the whole system, thus giving us purchase on the exploration of system-wide discontinuities, and individually – since what the simulations have revealed is that in the instances where there are two intersections, the position of the unstable intersection relative to the origin can be explored, and this has implications for the response of the system to different initial conditions. For example, if a particular $W_j^{initial}$ is nearer to the origin than the unstable point, then the system is more likely to 'jump' to the 'stable' zero at equilibrium, and vice versa. In this way, it may be possible to unpick path dependence. It should be possible to estimate plausible timelines for the exogenous variables and thus to reproduce the history of the evolution of retail systems. Explorations of alternatives would then lead us to search for discontinuities generated by changes in any of $\{e_i, P_i, c_{ij} \text{ or } K\}$.

The method can obviously be extended to other urban models. An obvious starting point for illustrative purposes is the Lowry (1964) model, and we pursue this avenue in Chapter 4. This illustrates discontinuities in the residential location sub-model and provides a basis for exploring the interdependence of the sub-models in a comprehensive model.

More detail can then be added to any of the sub-models. A residential location model disaggregated by social groups, for example, could be used to seek discontinuities that generate gentrification of city centres, for example, as will become clear in Chapter 4. We have argued that there are related systems that can be modelled using this kind of methodology (Wilson 2008). There are possible applications then in network analysis because this model system can be seen as a network generator.

Appendix 2.1 Notes about the dynamics

If we set the rent value K equal to the total spending power in the system divided by the total floor space in the system, it can be shown that the model will maintain the same overall floor space W at equilibrium as it had at the start of a model run. Because we are using a self-normalising model, we must also state that growth is coming from market capture from one zone over another.

Two forms of the retail dynamics equation have been used in previous research. The first we have used in this chapter:

$$\frac{dW_j}{dt} = \varepsilon\left(D_j - KW_j\right) \tag{2.7}$$

and a second variation is:

$$\frac{dW_j}{dt} = \varepsilon\left(D_j - KW_j\right)W_j \tag{2.8}$$

The second equation multiplies the value of ε by the W_j value of each retail zone, which is effectively reducing the rate at which small retail zones reach equilibrium. In some ways, this produces more realistic results; however, the time taken to reach equilibrium is so long that it is not practical to use it in an exploration of equilibrium structures. It can be shown using simulation that both equations produce almost identical equilibrium structures.

Appendix 2.2 Data sources

Residential zone spending power (e_iP_i) was calculated by multiplying together CAS ward-level population data from the UK 2001 census and average retail spending per month data derived from the ONS Family Spending 2010 Edition. The ward centre points were used as the location of each residential zone.

The retail zone data is from 2004 and comes from the Town Centres Project.

Notes

1   This bears out the conjecture in Wilson (1981) that there will be critical curves in (α, β) space.
2   This model, its best fit and all results derived from it are illustrative only because travel cost is represented by Euclidean distance rather than an accurate and detailed representation of the real transport network.

References

Addley, E. (2009) 'Empty, unlet and unloved: the new British high street', *Guardian*, 25 July 2009, p. 17.
Allen, P. M. and Sanglier, M. (1981) 'Urban evolution, self-organization, and decision making', *Environment and Planning A*, 13(2): 167–83.

Baker, R. G. V. (1994) 'An assessment of the space-time differential model for aggregate trip behaviour to planned suburban shopping centres', *Geographical Analysis*, 26(4): 341–62.

Batty, M. (1998) 'Urban evolution on the desktop: simulation with the use of extended cellular automata', *Environment and Planning A*, 30: 1943–67.

Batty, M. (2005) *Cities and Complexity: Understanding Cities with Cellular Automata, Agent-Based Models, and Fractals*, Cambridge, MA: MIT Press.

Batty, M. and Longley, P. (1994) *Fractal Cities: A Geometry of Form and Function*, San Diego, CA, and London: Academic Press.

Benguigui, L. and Czamanski, D. (2004) 'Simulation analysis of the fractality of cities', *Geographical Analysis*, 36(1): 69–85.

Borgers, A. W. J., Gunsing, M. and Timmermans, H. J. P. (1991) 'Teleshopping and the dynamics of urban retail systems: some numerical simulations', in D. Pumain (ed.), *Spatial Analysis and Population Dynamics*, Chantilly, France: John Libbey Eurotext, pp. 229–42.

Bura, S., Guérin-Pace, F., Mathian, H., Pumain, D. and Sanders, L. (1996) 'Multi-agents systems and the dynamics of a settlement system', *Geographical Analysis*, 28(2): 161–77.

Clarke, G. P., Clarke, M. and Wilson, A. G. (1986) 'Multiple bifurcation effects with a logistic attractiveness function in the supply side of a service system', *Systemi Urbani*, 7: 43–76.

Clarke, G. P., Langley, R. and Cardwell, W. (1998) 'Empirical applications of dynamic spatial interaction models', *Computers, Environmental and Urban Systems*, 22(2): 157–84.

Clarke, M. (1981) 'A note on the stability of equilibrium solutions of production constrained spatial interaction models', *Environment and Planning A*, 13: 601–5.

Clarke, M. and Wilson, A. G. (1985) 'The dynamics of urban spatial structure: the progress of a research programme', *Transactions, Institute of British Geographers*, 10: 427–51.

Dendrinos, D. S. and Mullally, H. (1981) 'Evolutionary patterns of urban populations', *Geographical Analysis*, 13(4): 328–44.

Feiner, S. and Beshers, C. (1990) 'Worlds within worlds: metaphors for exploring n-dimensional cirtual worlds', in *3rd Annual ACM SIGGRAPH*, Utah, UT: Snowbird, pp. 76–83.

Fotheringham, S. and Knudsen, D. (1986) 'Modeling discontinuous change in retailing systems: extensions of the Harris-Wilson framework with results from a simulated urban retailing system', *Geographical Analysis*, 18(4): 295–312.

Harris, B. and Wilson, A. G. (1978) 'Equilibrium values and dynamics of attractiveness terms in production-constrained spatial-interaction models', *Environment and Planning A*, 10: 371–88.

Hunt, B. and Slater, A. (2009) *21st Century High Streets: A New Vision for Our Town Centres*, London: British Retail Consortium.

LeBlanc, J., Ward, M. O. and Wittels, N. (1990) 'Exploring n-dimensional databases', in *Proc. Visualization '90*, San Francisco, CA: Computer Society Press, pp. 230–9.

Lombardo, S. R. (1986) 'New developments of a dynamic urban retail model with reference to consumers' mobility and costs for developers', in D. A. Griffith and R. J. Haining (eds), *Transformations Through Space and Time*, Dordrecht: Martinus Nijhoff, pp. 192–208.

Lombardo, S., Petri, M. and Zotta, D. (2004) 'Intelligent gis and retail location dynamics: a multi agent system integrated with arcgis', *Computational Science and its Applications – Iccsa 2004, Pt 2 Lecture Notes In Computer Science*, 3044: 1046–56.

Lowry, I. S. (1964) *A Model of Metropolis*, Memorandum RM.4035 – RC, Santa Monica, CA: Rand Corporation.

Nijkamp, P. and Reggiani, A. (1987) 'Spatial interaction and discrete choice: statics and dynamics', in J. Hauer, H. Timmermans and N. Wrigley (eds), *Contemporary Developments in Quantitative Geography*, Dordrecht: Reidel, pp. 125–51.

Nijkamp, P. and Reggiani, A. (1988) 'Dynamic spatial interaction models: new directions', *Environment and Planning A*, 20: 1449–60.

Oppenheim, N. (1986) 'Dynamic forecasting of urban shopping travel', *Transportation Research B*, 20: 391–402.

Phiri, P. (1980) 'Calculation of the equilibrium configuration of shopping facility sizes', *Environment and Planning*, 12: 983–1000.

Rijk, F. J. A. and Vorst, A. C. F. (1983a) 'Equilibrium points in an urban retail model and their connection with dynamical systems', *Regional Science and Urban Economics*, 13: 383–99.

Rijk, F. J. A. and Vorst, A. C. F. (1983b) 'On the uniqueness and existence of equilibrium points in an urban retail model', *Environment and Planning A*, 15: 475–82.

Straussfogel, D. (1991) 'Modeling suburbanization as an evolutionary system dynamic', *Geographical Analysis*, 23(1): 1–23.

Thom, R. (1975), *Structural Stability and Morphogenesis*, Reading, MA: W. A. Benjamin.

Wilson, A. G. (1981) *Catastrophe Theory and Bifurcation: Applications to Urban and Regional Systems*, London: Croom Helm.

Wilson, A. G. (1988) 'Configurational analysis and urban and regional theory', *Systemi Urbani*, 10: 51–62.

Wilson, A. G. (2008) 'Boltzmann, Lotka and Volterra and spatial structural evolution: an integrated methodology for some dynamical systems', *Journal of the Royal Society, Interface*, 5: 865–71.

3 Exploring possible urban futures in a non-linear dynamics regime

3.1 Forecasting the future of path-dependent urban systems

It is useful to think of the possible development path of an urban system as a high-dimensional 'cone' to highlight the potential for it to quickly diverge into one of a vast array of possible futures. We can potentially use this idea to determine the likely envelope that contains the real future state of the system. As we have indicated, the 'cone' exists in the very high dimensional state space of the system.

We have seen in the preceding chapter that urban systems are complex and non-linear, and exhibit properties of multiple equilibria and path dependence. This makes model-based forecasting in a conventional sense impossible. Path dependence is a key concept, first explored by Arthur (1988), who showed that history can influence industrial location patterns if agglomeration economies affect that industry. Agglomeration is a form of positive feedback and allows the possibility of multiple solutions to the industrial location problem. More generally, any system that experiences positive feedback can experience path dependence. In a planning context, the traditional use of urban models has been for exploring 'what if?' questions – i.e. for a given set of plans, what is the outcome? This chapter shows how to interpret this goal given the consequences of non-linearity through a focus on path dependence.

Martin and Sunley (2006) highlight many problems with the current definition of path dependence, and make it clear that much more work is needed to understand the concept properly. They worry that current forms of modelling reduce it to a mathematical concept. In this chapter, we model path dependence and argue that our interpretation of it as a 'dependence on a sequence of initial conditions' facilitates an exploration of system behaviour that can be a useful counterpart to more qualitative work on historical path dependence.

The value of each of the variables and parameters of an urban model at one time constitute a point in state space. Since, typically, many variables and parameters will be needed for an adequate description, this will be a very high dimensional space. We also find it helpful to follow Wilson (2008) and to think of the initial conditions – that are either exogenous in the model or part of the slow dynamics[1] – as the 'DNA' of the system because these conditions largely determine the possible models of development. At each of a sequence of points in time, the state vector will constitute the initial conditions for the next step. There are then two ways in which we can construct what we will call the possibility cone of development: (1) we can introduce stochastic variation into the dynamics of each model run from some time t – thus generating a set of varying outcomes at time $t + 1$; and (2) we can vary the exogenous DNA in the initial conditions at time t to produce a range of outcomes at time $t + 1$. The envelope of the initial conditions at time t and the outcomes at $t + 1$ forms a section of the possibility cone. Again, it should be emphasised that this is a 'cone' in a high-dimensional space.

The initial conditions typically will not represent an equilibrium state of the system. However, at each point in time, there will be equilibrium states that will be influencing future development. That is, there will be basins of attraction for multiple solutions, particularly when positive feedback is present. There are then interesting questions to be explored. Which basins of attraction are within the possibility cone and which are not? In the case of 'not', and if such a state is a desirable one, is it possible to make an adjustment in the initial conditions that brings that attractor within the cone? That is potentially a perspective to be adopted by planners in a complex non-linear world. This is, in a way, asking the question, 'what can be achieved by planning?'. It relates to the way in which urban systems can become 'locked in' to a given development path by the initial conditions. In dynamical systems terms, this represents being stuck near to an undesired basin of attraction. An example in the UK might be the seaside towns that are in decline and are experiencing negative 'lock in' to a restricted set of possible futures. There is the potential here to explore what is necessary to break them out of a negative development path. If the initial 'structural' conditions can be thought of as the 'DNA' of the system, then we can think of aspects of planning as 'genetic planning' by analogy with 'genetic medicine'.

In Section 3.2, we explore in more detail how to construct and represent a possibility cone. We use an aggregate urban retail model as a demonstrator – first in Section 3.3 by introducing stochastic variation of the initial conditions, and then in Section 3.4 by tackling a hypothetical planning application.

3.2 Constructing the possibility cone of an urban system

We have noted that if we take a given urban system at a particular moment in time, then we can consider 'the underlying structural variables to be the urban analogues of DNA' (Wilson 2008). The physiology is the activity and development of the city – the fast dynamics predicted by the model – given the starting DNA. To define the cone in modelling terms, we need to make a distinction between the exogenous DNA that our model does not directly adjust and endogenous DNA that our model adjusts and predicts. The cone of development we are envisioning here can be thought of as a rapidly diverging set of possibilities starting from a single set of endogenous DNA. We can begin by thinking of the many possibilities as a tree (Figure 3.1), each level of which represents one step through time. Each 'point' in this diagram is, of course, symbolic because it represents a high-dimension state vector.

The root of the tree is the initial endogenous DNA representing the current state of the system of interest. A number of branches extend from the root node representing development paths of the system towards equilibrium. The branching, recall, is brought about in one (or both) of two ways: through noise, representing

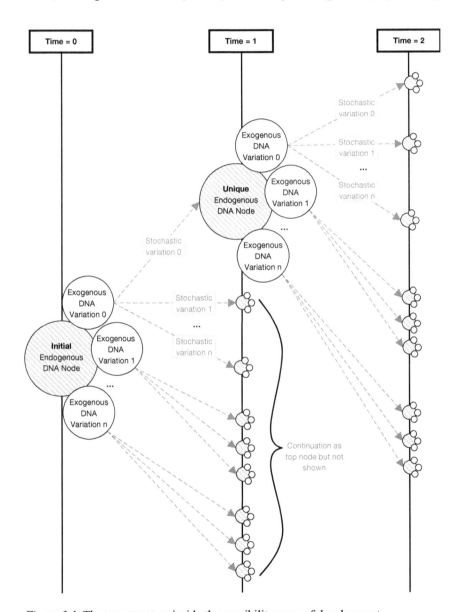

Figure 3.1 The tree structure inside the possibility cone of development

unpredictable events, or through adjustments to the exogenous DNA, which represent either a planned intervention, such as a new shopping centre or transport link, or an unplanned change, such as an increase or decrease in petrol prices. Generally, the planned interventions will be represented as a single binary choice at a specified time in the tree – either we build a new shopping centre or we do not. Unplanned changes would be represented by two or more branches that are allowed to occur at every time-step in the tree. One of the branches would be the 'no effect' option, while the other would represent each of the possible values that can have an effect on the system (e.g. fuel prices can increase, decrease or remain the same, and can do so at any point in time).

Computer software is used to recursively construct the tree. Starting with the root node, and for each child node following it in the tree at time t, we generate a number of branches equal to $(x_t * s)$, where x_t is the number of different exogenous DNA sets available at time-step t and s is the number of stochastically varying model runs we do with each exogenous DNA set. In order to represent the full range of potential variations, we would need to set s to a large value, and so, through time, the number of the branches in the tree will increase very rapidly. If m is the maximum time depth of the tree (numbered from zero), then the number of model runs required to construct the tree/cone N will be:

$$N = \sum_{t=0}^{m-1} \prod_{i=0}^{t} \left(x_i * s \right) \tag{3.1}$$

Clearly, a significant amount of computing power would be required to construct a deep cone for anything other than the simplest of models.

Each tree branch represents one model run from a complete DNA set at time t, and this may or may not be iterated to equilibrium. The output from the model run represents a new and unique endogenous DNA set that forms a new node in the tree at the end of the branch. By choosing a path through the tree from the root to a leaf node, we can see that the tree represents a wide range of possible development paths that cover a number of time-steps. The envelope of this process is the cone of possible development.

Dealing with stochastic variation is relatively straightforward, and we give an example in the next section. In the case of changes to the exogenous DNA, we can build a set of varying exogenous DNA for each time-step in the tree. Each of these exogenous DNA will represent one permutation of the events that could possibly occur at the time-step in question. An example set of future events that could occur at some time-step t could be: fuel price fluctuations, planned development of a new shopping centre and construction of a new road. The exogenous DNA set we generate from this would then include every permutation of the three events (Table 3.1), and can be thought of as a set of possible future scenarios for the system at time t. Computer software can obviously be used to automatically generate these sets, given the set of possible events.

It is easy to see that if we move from a narrow set of highly probable events to including increasingly unlikely events, the possibility cone will grow and will

Table 3.1 Example exogenous DNA variation set for one time-step

Exogenous DNA index	Fuel prices	Shopping centre	Road
0	Increase	Not built	Not built
1	Increase	Not built	Built
2	Increase	Built	Not built
3	Increase	Built	Built
4	No change	Not built	Not built
5	No change	Not built	Built
6	No change	Built	Not built
7	No change	Built	Built
8	Decrease	Not built	Not built
9	Decrease	Not built	Built
10	Decrease	Built	Not built
11	Decrease	Built	Built

be more likely to contain the real future state of the system. A balance needs to be struck, however, because there are obvious limits on the resources of time and computing power available to construct such a cone.

3.3 A stochastic version of the aggregate retail model

To construct a realistic possibility cone of development for a given urban system would require a comprehensive model that represented multiple subsystems and the interdependencies that exist between them. For the purposes of demonstrating the techniques, we concentrate in this study on modelling a single subsystem – urban retail – however, the approach could be applied to more comprehensive models, and this is an intended area of future research.

We use the archetypal aggregate retail model developed by Harris and Wilson (1978), and first discussed in Chapter 1. The usual variables for a retail demonstrator are defined again here for convenience. There are retail zones, j, and we define W_j as the amount of retail floor space in each such zone; this value also represents the attractiveness of that retail zone to consumers. We also define a number of residential zones, i, with population, P_i, and average spending power, e_i. The combined spending power of all the consumers in residential zone i is $e_i P_i$. The cost of travelling from zone i to zone j is given by c_{ij}. The accessibility of each retail zone is represented by an additional multiplier, m_j, which affects every travel cost c_{ij} into retail zone j. This allows us to roughly represent a varying accessibility of zones caused by a complicated transport network without resorting to a full detailed representation. The parameter α represents returns to scale, so we expect path dependence wherever this parameter is greater than 1, representing increasing returns to scale, and giving rise to the possibility of multiple solutions. The β parameter represents the impact of travel cost on consumer shopping decisions. In this case, the exogenous variables are $\{m_j\}$, e_i, P_i, and the model will predict W_j as the 'slow dynamics'. The interaction array $\{S_{ij}\}$ constitutes the fast dynamics. The DNA, therefore, is:

$$[\{m_j\}, \{e_i\}, \{P_i\}, \{W_j\}, \alpha, \beta]$$

The flow of consumer spending from residential zone i to retail zone j is given in the usual way by:

$$S_{ij} = A_i e_i P_i W_j^{\alpha} \exp\left(-\beta c_{ij}\right) \tag{3.2}$$

where:

$$A_i = \frac{1}{\sum_k W_k^{\alpha} \exp\left(-\beta c_{ik}\right)} \tag{3.3}$$

to ensure that:

$$\sum_j S_{ij} = e_i P_i \tag{3.4}$$

we can calculate the total flows into destinations as:

$$D_j = \sum_i S_{ij} = \sum_i \frac{e_i P_i W_j^{\alpha} \exp\left(-\beta c_{ij}\right)}{\sum_k W_k^{\alpha} \exp\left(-\beta c_{ik}\right)} \tag{3.5}$$

The usual hypothesis for representing the dynamics is:

$$\frac{dW_j}{dt} = \varepsilon\left(D_j - KW_j\right) \tag{3.6}$$

In order to represent the random events that can affect path dependence, we add a stochastic term to the dynamics to give:

$$\Delta W_j = \varepsilon\left(D_j - KW_j\right) + W_j \varphi \tag{3.7}$$

where ϕ is a stochastic[2] term drawn from a normal distribution with a mean (σ) of zero and a standard deviation of 0.04. This results in a low level of noise in the system that is proportional to the size of the retail zone. This is an assumption we make based on the idea that the larger the number of retail units in a zone, the greater the potential for unpredictable change. This also keeps the total amount of stochastic variation in the system roughly constant (due to a constant total amount of floor space in the system).

The iterative process represents the system converging towards an equilibrium state; however, we choose here to explicitly represent the passage of time as a single step from a set of initial W_j values to the set of W_j values that exist at the end of a model run. Rather than running the model to equilibrium, each model run lasts for 200 iterations. This represents the idea that while a system might evolve towards a particular equilibrium state, it may not reach it if some external change (random or planned) causes a change in the phase space of the system.

In order to make the structure of the resulting possibility cone accessible for both analysis and communication purposes, we visualise its structure. We are effectively plotting the tree from Figure 3.1 in the multidimensional state space of the system. Each node in the tree represents a $\{W_j\}$. This obviously presents some challenges because it is a high-dimensional structure and contains a lot of information. Parallel coordinates (d'Ocagne 1885; Inselberg 1985) are one of the clearest and most intuitive of the multidimensional visualisation techniques available. Here, we use a parallel coordinates plot at each time-step to display the range of stable states reached by the various trajectories that have been calculated.

We demonstrate the techniques developed so far by constructing and visualising a simple possibility cone for the metropolitan county of South Yorkshire in the UK containing 19 retail zones and 94 residential zones (data sources as in Chapter 2). This example is only intended as a proof of concept and not as a case study from which conclusions should be drawn about the nature of the real system.

A map showing the region is given in Figure 3.2. The heights of the bars in the figure illustrate the initial $\{W_j\}$ that represents the initial endogenous DNA for our possibility cone. The exogenous DNA used to build the cone was found by calibrating the model to produce the closest equilibrium solution to the initial conditions data. The travel cost matrix $\{c_{ij}\}$ is calculated from shortest paths through the road network (see Appendix 3.1 for construction details and data sources).

In order to make this first example as simple as possible, we keep the exogenous DNA constant and rely on stochastic variation to differentiate each model run. We also model only a single time-step into the future. To reiterate, in the terminology of Equation 3.1, we set $s = 100$, $m = 1$, $x_0 = 1$ to produce a cone with 100 nodes branching out from a single initial root node, each of which represents one model run. The resulting cone of development can be seen in Figure 3.3.

The figure shows three parallel coordinates plots. Figure 3.3a is a shaded envelope that contains the end result of all model runs. The varying width of this shows how the impact of noise varies between retail centres. The black line running horizontally across the shaded area indicates the size of each centre in the initial conditions data from 2004. The axes are scaled to total amount of floor space in the system. Some centres, such as Sheffield, are stable within a small range relative to their size, while other centres, such as Doncaster, vary a lot.

Figure 3.3b shows the end state of all 100 model runs over-plotted using spline-based parallel coordinates. The plotted lines are translucent so the dark areas of the plot, indicating areas that many end states pass through. This technique allows the relationship between neighbouring centres in the diagram to be identified. A very strong market-capture-type relationship can be seen between Parkgate and Rotherham, and also between Doncaster and Doncaster Lakeside. With interactive reordering of the axes, all relationships in the system can be explored.

Figure 3.3c shows how brushing can be used to get around the problem of over-plotting and obscuring individual model runs. Brushed splines are highlighted in

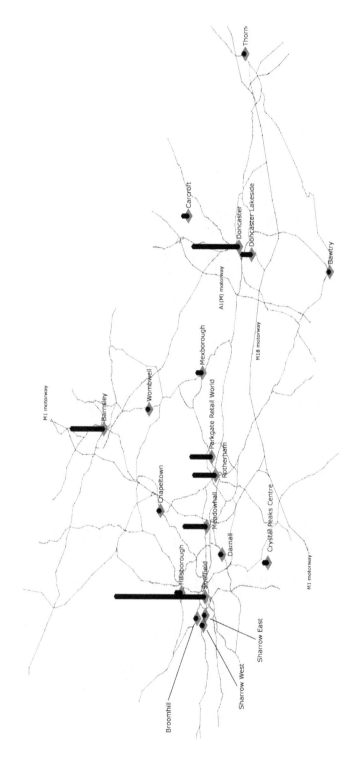

Figure 3.2 Modelled region of South Yorkshire showing retail zones and road network (contains Ordnance Survey data © Crown copyright and database right 2014, www.ordnancesurvey.co.uk/docs/licences/os-opendata-licence.pdf)

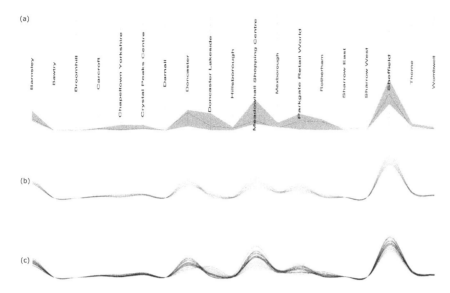

Figure 3.3 Single-stage cone of development for South Yorkshire: (a) envelope
containing all end states, (b) detail of end states and (c) brushed detail in
plot showing impact of Meadowhall growing large

a heavier black line. By brushing the top 50 per cent of the range of possible sizes
of Meadowhall, we can see that this corresponds to the bottom 60 per cent of the
range of possible sizes at Sheffield.

This kind of prediction is really giving us an idea of the pressures that exist on
each retail centre, be it growth or decline, and where these pressures come from.
How planners, developers and retailers respond to these pressures would then
determine the evolutionary path of the system.

3.4 Tackling a hypothetical planning application

We now add an additional layer of complexity by adding variation to the
exogenous DNA. We can use this to represent both deliberate planned changes
and unplanned events that may or may not occur. Within the constraints of the
retail model we are using, we can model the following unplanned events:

- fuel price fluctuations (affecting the β parameter);
- migration (affecting P_i); and
- recession and expansion of the economy (potentially affecting both e_i and β).

It is interesting to note that these are generally occurrences that are out of the
hands of planners, representing changes caused by the global economy, major
technological improvement and potentially even climate change. Deliberate
planned events we can model include:

1   rail and bus network construction and road construction (causing an adjustment in the c_{ij} and/or $\{m_j\}$);
2   retail zone construction (increasing a particular W_j);
3   housing construction (affecting P_i if we assume the houses are used); and
4   changes in taxation (affecting e_i).

We use the South Yorkshire region as our test case again, and for simplicity's sake consider one planned event and one unplanned event. We take the planned event as the construction of Sheffield's New Retail Quarter – a scheme that plans to add ~65,000 m² of retail to the city by 2018. The unplanned event will be petrol price fluctuations. Details of these events are given in Table 3.2.

The planned cone of development will contain three time-steps with the construction of the additional retail capacity on time-step 2. From these events, we can generate a set of varying exogenous DNA for each time-step in the cone.

Again following the methodology given in Section 3.2, we set $s = 3$, $m = 3$, $x_0 = 3$, $x_1 = 6$, $x_2 = 3$, giving a tree constructed from 1,629 model runs and representing 1,458 different development paths. Figure 3.5 shows the resulting cone of development.

Figure 3.5a shows a shaded area that contains the end point of all model runs. Although this cone is a longer timeline and contains more variation in the exogenous parameter sets than the cone in Figure 3.3, it has not widened a great deal except at Meadowhall. Sheffield and Barnsley in the west of the region are the two most stable large centres. Meadowhall, Parkgate, Rotherham and Doncaster all vary much more widely, possibly because of the mix of old and new centres. Figure 3.5b shows all the end states without the New Retail Quarter and Figure 3.5c shows all the end states with the New Retail Quarter. There is very little difference in the predicted outcomes, suggesting that this is a beneficial development that would not impact negatively on other centres. Figure 3.5d shows the detail available on brushing the individual model run end state splines. In this case, it shows that Meadowhall growing very large increases the likelihood of decline in the surrounding centres, especially Parkgate Retail World.

3.5 Conclusions

We have demonstrated a method for constructing and visualising the multi-dimensional possibility cone of development for an urban system. Such a technique

Table 3.2 Details of possible future events represented in the possibility cone

Event name	Timing	Parameter options
Retail expansion	Time-step 2	$W_{Sheffield}$ unmodified $W_{Sheffield}$ +65,000
Petrol price fluctuation	Every time-step	β unmodified β +0.1 β −0.1

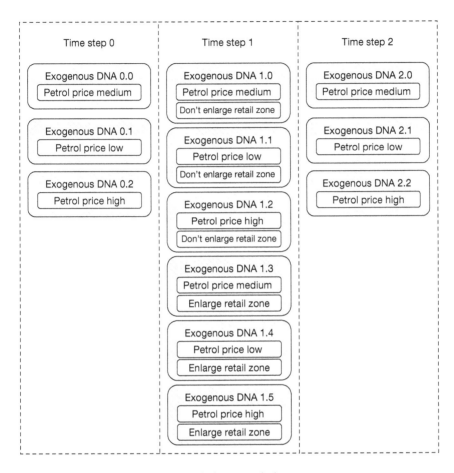

Figure 3.4 The exogenous DNA variation at each time-step

provides a useful way of approaching urban planning and specifically forecasting the future of non-deterministic complex urban systems. For planners, the implications of this idea is that the possibility cone represents a way of identifying those system states within reach, and discontinuous change from one stable state to another represents a possible path creation mechanism.

Here, we have focused on retail in order to simplify our initial explorations; however, to gain a full understanding of the possibility cone of urban development, a more comprehensive model would be required. This presents a range of challenges due to the computing power required to build the cone. The output is also likely to be far more complex than the system demonstrated here, making visualisation even more challenging.

The idea that a system moves between the basin of attraction of a number of solutions is a useful way of thinking about path dependence, and future research might look for ways to map out and visualise these multidimensional structures.

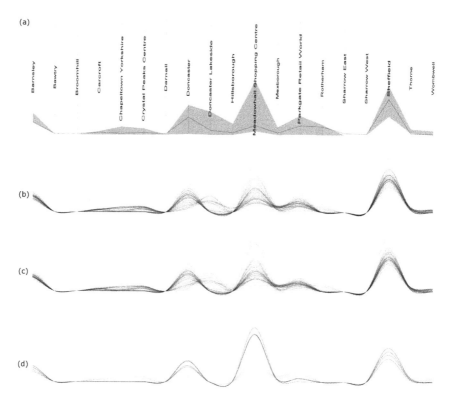

Figure 3.5 Three-stage cone of development with exogenous variation for a hypothetical planning application in South Yorkshire: (a) envelope containing all end states, (b) detail of end states for evolutionary paths without the New Retail Quarter, (c) detail of end states for evolutionary paths with the New Retail Quarter and (d) brushed detail in plot showing impact of Meadowhall growing very large

Appendix 3.1 Transport network details

Meridian 2 data (http://data.gov.uk/dataset/meridian-2) was used for the motorways and A-roads. Minor roads were generated by triangulating the vertices of the whole network. This was necessary because the location of each retail centre is the centroid of an area and not exact enough to connect up with the real minor roads. The value of m_j was set to 1 for all retail zones except Parkgate Retail World and Doncaster Lakeside, which used values 0.95 and 0.98 to represent the fact that they are retail parks with 2,000 and 950 free parking spaces, respectively. Meadowhall Shopping Centre's location at a motorway junction meant lowering its m_j value from 1 was not necessary to have the model fit, despite it having 12,000 free parking spaces.

Notes

1 'Fast dynamics' variables, such as interaction arrays, will be calculated within the model and should not be thought of as part of the DNA.
2 We use the Mersenne Twister algorithm to generate uniformly distributed random numbers (Matsumoto and Nishimura 1998). These are then transformed into random numbers from a Gaussian distribution using the polar form of the Box-Müller algorithm (Box and Müller 1958).

References

Arthur, W. B. (1988) 'Urban systems and historical path dependence', in J. H. Ausubel and R. Herman (eds), *Cities and Their Vital Systems: Infrastructure, Past, Present and Future*, Washington, DC: National Academy Press, pp. 85–97.

Box, G. E. P. and Müller, M. E. (1958) 'A note on the generation of random normal deviates', *The Annals of Mathematical Statistics*, 29(2): 610–11.

d'Ocagne, M. (1885) *Coordonnées Parallèles Et Axiales-Méthode De Transformation Géométrique Et Procédé Nouveau De Calcul Graphique Déduit De La Considération Des Coordonnées Parallèles*, Paris: Gauthier-Villars.

Harris, B. and Wilson, A. G. (1978) 'Equilibrium values and dynamics of attractiveness terms in production-constrained spatial-interaction models', *Environment and Planning A*, 10: 371–88.

Inselberg, A. (1985) 'The plane with parallel coordinates', *The Visual Computer*, 1(2): 69–91.

Martin, R. and Sunley, P. (2006) 'Path dependence and regional economic evolution', *Journal of Economic Geography*, 6(4): 395–437.

Matsumoto, M. and Nishimura, T. (1998) 'Mersenne twister: a 623-dimensionally equidistributed uniform pseudo-random number generator', *ACM Transactions on Modeling and Computer Simulation*, 8(1): 3–30.

Wilson, A. (2008) *Urban and Regional Dynamics–3: 'DNA' and 'Genes' as a Basis for Constructing a Typology of Areas*, CASA Working Paper, London: Centre for Advanced Spatial Analysis (UCL).

4 A dynamic comprehensive model

4.1 The Lowry model

The Lowry model (Lowry 1964) has rightly achieved iconic status because it represented the main ideas that would underpin any comprehensive urban model in the simplest possible way. It could then be progressively refined, and many authors have contributed to this programme. It is deployed here as an underpinning framework to illustrate a new development. While many of the post-Lowry models are dynamic, none, to our knowledge, employ the kind of mechanism that has been tested in the context of the retail model – used in preceding chapters. This approach makes non-linearities in the different Lowry-type sub-models explicit, and, as we know, one of the properties of such models is the possibility of phase changes – abrupt changes in elements of spatial structure at some critical parameter values. We show, as an example in this case, that this allows us to represent the gentrification process. The context for the model presented here, therefore, consists of the Lowry model itself and the dynamic retail model, the concepts of which can then be extended into other sub-models.

The main variables in the original Lowry model are:

- A = area of land
- E = employment
- P = population
- c = trip cost
- Z = constraints

to which should be added the following to be used as subscripts or superscripts:

- U = unusable land
- B = basic sector
- R = retail sector
- H = household sector
- k = class of establishment within a sector
- m = number of classes of retail establishment
- i, j = zones
- n = number of zones

So, A_i^H, for example, is the area of land in zone i that is used for housing. If a subscript or a superscript is omitted, this implies summation. So, A_i, for example, is the total amount of land in i. There are two kinds of economic sector: basic and retail – the latter further subdivided. Basic employment – and its spatial distribution across zones – is given exogenously. Retail employment is generated by the population. Once this simple principle of building the variables – the region's descriptors – is understood, the 12 equations of the model can be presented.

The key land use equation is:

$$A_j^H = A_j - A_j^U - A_j^B - A_j^R \tag{4.1}$$

In this equation, he captured some key hypotheses, in effect saying that land for basic and retail industries can always outbid housing, so this shows land available for housing is a residual.

The household sector is represented by:

$$P = f \sum_j E_j \tag{4.2\}}$$

$$P_j = g \sum_i E_i f_{\text{res}}\left(c_{ij}\right) \tag{4.3}$$

$$\sum_j P_j = P \tag{4.4}$$

$$P_j \leq z^H A_j^H \tag{4.5}$$

This sequence generates the population from employment and begins the process of housing them. The first (Equation 4.2) calculates total population as proportional to total employment. The second (Equation 4.3) allocates this population to zones, $i. f_{\text{res}}(c_{ij})$ is a declining function of travel cost from i to j, thus building in the likelihood that workers live nearer to their workplace. The third equation (Equation 4.4) enables g in Equation 4.3 to be calculated as a normalising factor. The fourth equation (Equation 4.5) is particularly interesting and also shows how the model is more complicated than appears at first sight. z^H is the unit amount of land used for residences, and so this equation is constraining the numbers assigned to zone i in relation to land availability. This is one of the subtleties – and part of the trickiness – of the model: the equations have to be solved iteratively to ensure that this constraint is satisfied.

The retail sector is represented by:

$$E^{Rk} = a^k P \tag{4.6}$$

$$E_j^{Rk} = b^k \left[c^k \sum_i P_i f^k\left(c_{ij}\right) + d^k E_j \right] \tag{4.7}$$

$$\sum_j E_j^{Rk} = E^{Rk} \tag{4.8}$$

$$E_j^{Rk} > z^{Rk} \tag{4.9}$$

$$A_j^R = \sum_k e^k E_j^{Rk} \tag{4.10}$$

$$A_j^R \le A_j - A_j^U - A_j^B \tag{4.11}$$

These six equations determine the amount of employment generated in the retail sector. The total in sector k within retail is given by the first equation (Equation 4.6), and this is spatially distributed through the second (Equation 4.7). As with the residential location equation, the function $f^k(c_{ij})$ is a decreasing function of travel cost, indicating that retail facilities will be demanded relatively nearer to residences. c^k converts these units into employment. The term $d^k E_j$ represents use of retail facilities from the workplace. b^k is a normalising factor that can be determined from Equation 4.8. Equation 4.9 imposes a minimum size for retail sector k at a location. (No school for half a dozen pupils, for example!) Equations 4.10 and 4.11 sort out retail land use, the first calculating a total from a sum of k-sector uses – e^k converting employment into land – and the second specifying the maximum amount of retail land – in effect, giving 'basic' (which has been given exogenously) priority over retail. In this case, unlike the residential case, where P_i was constrained by land availability, retail employment is not so constrained. Lowry argued that, if necessary, retail could 'build upwards'. If A_j^R from Equation 4.10 exceeds $A_j - A_j^U - A_j^B$, it is reset to this maximum, but employment does not change.

Total employment is then given by:

$$E_j = E_j^B + \sum_k E_j^{Rk} \tag{4.12}$$

This final equation simply adds up the total employment in each zone. The equations are solved iteratively, starting with $E_j^{Rk} = 0$. As we have noted, the model is quite sophisticated in the way it uses constraints to handle land use, and it is also a useful illustration of something we need always to bear in mind in model design – the distinction between exogenous and endogenous variables. In this case, the given location of basic employment is the exogenous driver but the $\{c_{ij}\}$ array can also be seen as reflecting the (exogenously specified) investment in transport.

We now introduce this mechanism not only into Lowry's retail model, but also into his residential location model. In the next section, we present this extended model and then show how it can be used to represent phase changes.

4.2 The Lowry model with full dynamics

4.2.1 Introduction

We build a model that works through a number of steps. Each of these represents a unit of time and movement towards equilibrium with a relatively slow relaxation time for the system. We use similar industry categories to the Lowry model but differentiate consumer-driven service industries from those that can be thought to be regulated – such as education and health. This provides a basis for more effective use of the model in planning. The industry categories are:

- basic industry;
- consumer-driven service industries; and
- regulated service industries.

The unregulated services represented are retail and a catch-all 'other consumer driven services' category. The regulated service industries represented are health and education.

The initial conditions for the original Lowry model used only basic industry employment data, from which it developed the rest of a city. We seek both to make the model more relevant to mature regions and to explore path dependence by starting with initial conditions that represent the current land use mix and are generated using the following zone-level data:

- employment by industry;
- population by income level; and
- average house price by type.

In this way, we begin to introduce additional levels of disaggregation, which will ultimately make such models more realistic. However, like the Lowry model, the assumption is made that basic industry is the driver of growth. In Dearden (2012), timelines are explored in which basic employment is exogenously changed over the course of a model run. BLV-type dynamics are used to model changes in unregulated service provision, housing provision and house prices. Regulated service industries are adjusted to match overall population change. Each of these subsystems is described in its own section below.

4.2.2 System overview

Figure 4.1 shows the steps involved in each time-step of the model. The model moves through updating basic industry, updating regulated services to match population growth, updating unregulated services and then updating the residential location and housing model. Inner iterative loops are used to ensure that growth in basic employment and growth in regulated service provision matches a prescribed rate regardless of how land is constrained in the region.

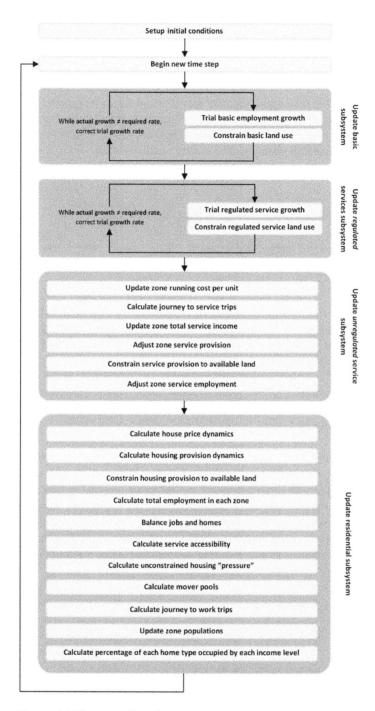

Figure 4.1 Time-step flow diagram

It was noted briefly above that, in addition to incorporating explicit dynamics, a more detailed level of disaggregation is adopted. The key additional levels are: housing type (k), person type, particularly with respect to income (w), service type (x), and employment by x and w. The variables and indices are listed in Tables 4.1–4.4 in Appendix 4.1 – exogenous and endogenous variables, and indices in turn.

4.2.3 Land constraints

The system of land constraints used here differs from that used by Lowry. The assumption in the original model, as we have seen, is that certain land use types take priority over others – basic industry first, then retail, and, lastly, residential. The Lowry model enforced density constraints and minimum service centre sizes. If these were not met, then the surplus provision from constrained zones was reallocated to zones that had not yet exceeded these constraints. In our case, because the model is dynamic, there are many different factors affecting the amount of each different land use in a zone. Each time-step follows on from that in the previous time-step (in contrast to Lowry, who reset them at each iteration). In a dynamic model such as this, maintaining realistic rates of change is a requirement. As a result of all this, land constraints are more difficult to apply. To deal with this, the simplest possible solution was taken. There is no mechanism for one land use type to displace another, so the subsystems compete for land on a first come, first served basis. As a result, growth of any land use that would exceed the available land is constrained to fit in the available land. The details are presented in Dearden (2012). Clearly, this is just one approach to representing this complicated mechanism in a dynamic model, and future research could develop this further.

4.2.4 Basic industry

A basic employment growth rate is set for each time-step (uniform across the region). If this causes the land constraints in a zone to be exceeded, then the total amount of basic industry is constrained in that zone and the 'surplus' growth is redistributed. The detailed mechanism is in Dearden (2012). This process generates $\{E_i^B\}$.

4.2.5 Regulated service industry sub-model

The evolution of regulated services, such as health and education, is often planned rather than determined in a market. Here, a simple assumption is made that a given initial service provision will grow proportionately with changes in the regional population. The initial growth rate matches the last percentage change in the system population. Then a similar mechanism is used to constrain land use as that described for basic employment. Alternatively, these variables can be set exogenously to represent planned change.

This process generates $\{W_j^x\}$ and $\{E_i^x\}$ for regulated services.

The unregulated – retail and other consumer driven – services are represented using the standard BLV retail model framework. For each of these in turn, the following steps are run through:

(1) First, the rent for unregulated services x in each zone K_j^x is calculated based on the accessibility to population (workers and non-workers) scaled by a constant, γ.

(2) Service usage trips S_{ij}^{xw} are calculated between each pair of zones for each person type.

(3) An inverse activity rate is used to include demand from non-workers in these calculations.

(4) The key step is now to introduce explicit dynamics. Total service revenue D_j^x attracted to each zone and unit area costs K_j^x are used to calculate the change in unregulated service provision ΔW_j^x:

$$D_j^x = \sum_{iw} S_{ij}^{xw} \tag{4.13}$$

$$\Delta W_j^x = \varepsilon^x \left(D_j^x - K_j^x W_j^x \right) \tag{4.14}$$

The term in brackets is the level of profit for the service in the zone.

(5) If these changes cause the land constraints in a zone to be exceeded, then the total land used by the unregulated service industries is constrained in that zone.

(6) This process generates $\{W_j^x\}$ for unregulated services, and the change in employment can then be calculated.

4.2.7 Residential location sub-model

The residential location sub-model is the most complex of the sub-models. It is disaggregated by three home types (small, large and temporary) and three resident income groups (low, medium and high).

(1) First, change in house price Δh_i^k is calculated based on the difference between the housing provision H_i^k and housing pressure L_i^k:

$$\Delta h_i^k = \varphi_1 \left[L_i^k - H_i^k \right] \tag{4.15}$$

In the first time-step, it is assumed that housing pressure is equal to housing provision so there is no change. In later time-steps, the housing pressure calculated in the previous time-step is used. As we will see, we need to construct temporary housing (described later) as part of a mechanism to balance available jobs and available homes. The 'price' of temporary housing is assumed to be static $\Delta h_i^{temporary}$. A similar system is used to calculate change in housing provision H_i^k on a fully dynamic basis:

$$\Delta H_i^k = \varphi_2 \left[L_i^k - H_i^k \right] \tag{4.16}$$

(2) Next, total employment in each zone is disaggregated by income group, w. A requirement of the journey to work model (described later) is that the number of jobs and homes in the region is balanced.

(3) Combined accessibility to services Z_i^w is used as a simple representation of the residential attractiveness of a particular zone. This is calculated and used in an employment-constrained journey to work model U_{ij}^{kw} to calculate housing pressure L_i^k. This gives us a measure of where residents would ideally live and work if there were no constraints on housing provision. Temporary housing is excluded from these calculations to ensure that 'real' housing is constructed to make up any shortfall.

(4) To calculate residential location, a spatial interaction model based on the one described by Wilson (1974: 187) is used. The version shown here differs in that disaggregation by householder status (head of household or not)[1] has been removed and feedback has been introduced into the model to allow the rate of change to be controlled by the relative sizes of the four mover pools in the model. The mover pools are defined as:

1   people changing home and employment;
2   people changing employment only;
3   people changing home only; and
4   people changing neither home or employment.

(5) These flows are aggregated to calculate the new population of workers in each zone, P_i^w, and the new population of workers and non-workers Q_i^w using the inverse activity rate σ.

4.3 Running the model as an interactive, visual computer simulation

4.3.1 Introduction

South Yorkshire was used as an example region to test the model. The region is divided into 212 zones, each of which is 3 km² (Figure 4.2). The data sources used to generate the initial conditions are detailed in Appendix 4.3. Custom software was developed in C++ to allow a user to run the model and visualise each time-step.

Equilibrium is defined as no change greater than 0.1 per cent in any endogenous variable for at least 100 time-steps. This allows automatic detection of when the model reaches an equilibrium solution and provides a consistent stopping condition for the model runs. Given that this model contains so many degrees of freedom, an automatic calibration system would likely take a huge amount of time to run, so the calibration was done manually using intuition about the realistic values that the parameters might take. A useful starting point for the retail subsystem was the previous best-fit parameters found for South Yorkshire in previous work (Dearden and Wilson 2011). Interactive visualisation also helped in this process

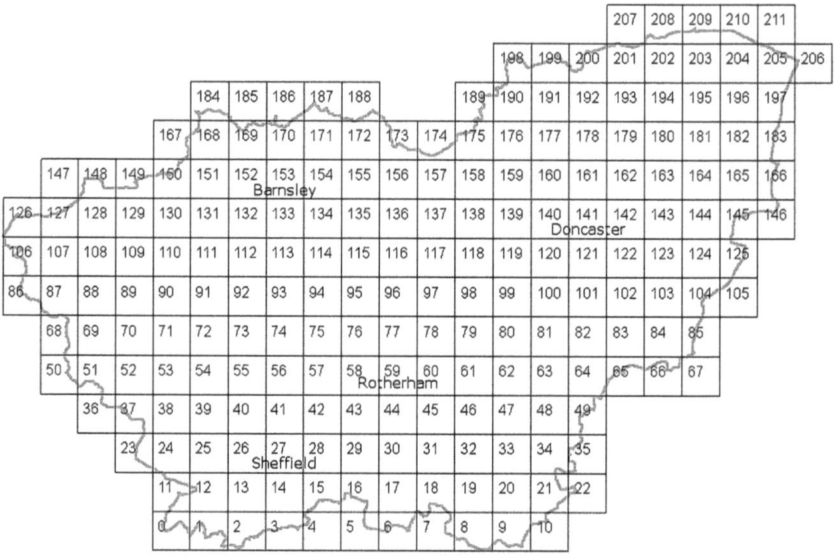

Figure 4.2 Zone system for South Yorkshire labelled with zone indices and main settlements

because the dynamics of the model could be explored – played back many times – to better understand why the model was deviating from a good fit. The variables against which the model is calibrated are those endogenous variables predicted by the dynamic BLV and mover-pool type subsystems:

- unregulated service provision by service type;
- total population by income level;
- home price by housing type; and
- home provision by housing type.

4.3.2 Results grids around best fit

A two-dimensional results grid is generated around the best-fit parameter set. The grid varies the following two parameters:

- α, varying from 0.9 to 1.2 in steps of 0.05: representing the impact of service centre size on consumer service usage decisions.
- τ, varying from –0.05 to +0.05 in steps of 0.05: representing an addition/subtraction to the impact of travel cost for both journey to work decisions (β) and journey to service decisions (μ) for all income groups. So τ represents a change in the cost of travel and is assumed to affect journeys of all types in a similar way.

In the case of the retail model, it was possible to develop a basic results grid to facilitate calibration and identification of discontinuities in a single subsystem. In this case, there are many linked subsystems that make both calibration and the identification of discontinuities more difficult. A discontinuity in one subsystem has the potential to cause discontinuities in other subsystems.

The model was run until equilibrium was detected for each cell in the grid, as described at the beginning of Section 4.3. Figures 4.3–4.9 each display a results grid for one of the six fast-changing[2] endogenous variables. The main settlements in the real system are marked with a line for easy comparison across the grid. The results grids for the unregulated services (retail in Figure 4.6 and other consumer-driven services in Figure 4.7) show clear lines along which both single and multiple zone discontinuities occur. One example for other consumer-driven services in Figure 4.7 is from (1.1, –0.05) to (1.2, –0.05). Here, a medium-sized centre to the east of Sheffield is replaced by a large centre to the north of Sheffield. The $\alpha = 1$ discontinuity demonstrated for retail in earlier chapters is not visible, most likely due to the fact that the impact of travel cost on journey to service decisions is not set low enough for this to appear (recall this transition only appeared at low beta values for the retail model in earlier chapters). Figures 4.3–4.5 show how moving from low alpha and theta to high alpha and theta causes the competition for housing in large settlements to increase. In this case, the higher income groups move to the centre of the large settlements and the lower income groups are displaced to the edge – Doncaster being the clearest example of this

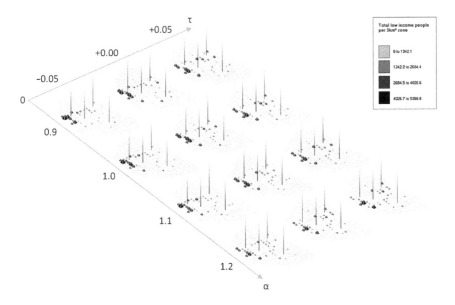

Figure 4.3 (α, τ) results for grid for low-income population; the main settlements in the real system are marked with a line for easy comparison across the grid

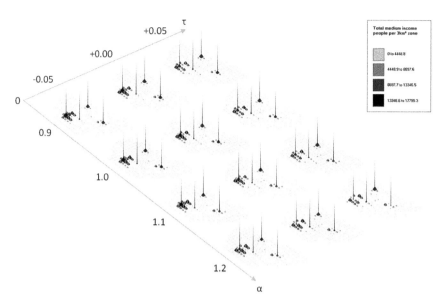

Figure 4.4 (α, τ) results for grid for medium-income population; the main
settlements in the real system are marked with a line for easy
comparison across the grid

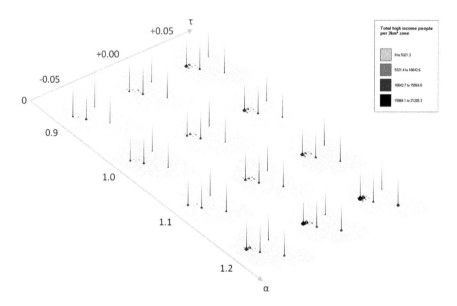

Figure 4.5 (α, τ) results for grid for high-income population; the main settlements
in the real system are marked with a line for easy comparison across
the grid

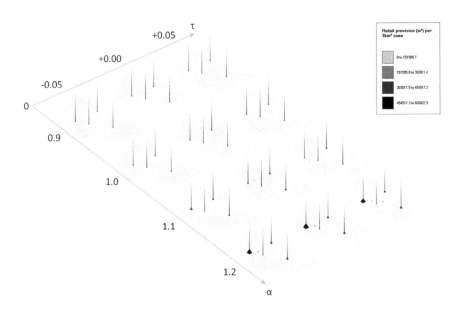

Figure 4.6 (α, τ) results for grid for retail; the main settlements in the real system are marked with a line for easy comparison across the grid

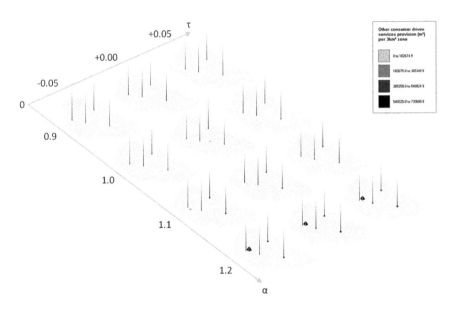

Figure 4.7 (α, τ) results for grid for other consumer-driven services; the main settlements in the real system are marked with a line for easy comparison across the grid

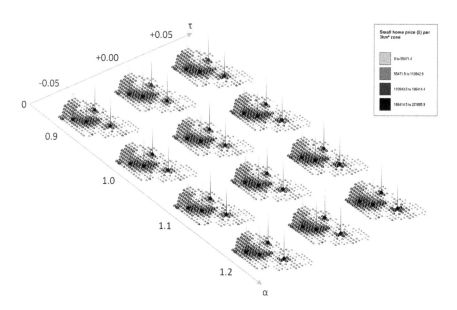

Figure 4.8 (α, τ) results for grid for small home price; the main settlements in the real system are marked with a line for easy comparison across the grid

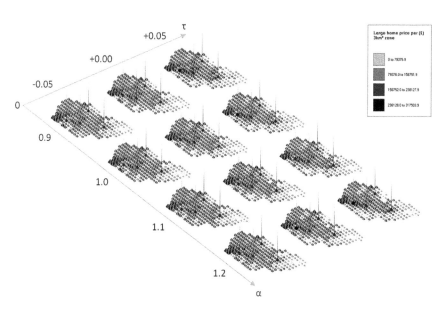

Figure 4.9 (α, τ) results for grid for large home price; the main settlements in the real system are marked with a line for easy comparison across the grid

in the grid because it is furthest away from the other large settlements. House prices show less obvious patterns across the grid, but there is a general trend for house prices to increase near large settlements as travel cost increases.

4.4 Discontinuities in the residential model: the onset of gentrification

The methods for gaining insights into discontinuities in retail systems are well understood and have been described in earlier chapters. In order to analyse those in other subsystems, and particularly the residential one, it will be appropriate to develop a zone graph similar to the one developed for the retail model. In the retail zone graph, the quantities plotted were the revenues and costs in the BLV dynamics equation. The residential subsystem in this model contains BLV-type dynamics for house price and housing provision, and these could potentially be analysed using a zone graph. The situation here is different from the retail case because there are two residential location dynamics equations (Equations 4.15 and 4.16) rather than one. Also, in the retail zone graph, one of the quantities, the running cost, KW_j, produces a constant straight line. In the residential case, both the quantities in the dynamics equation (housing pressure by housing type, L_i^k, and housing provision by housing type, H_i^k) are non-linear.

As a starting point, a residential zone graph specific to one housing type is developed. This plots zone house price for housing type k, h_i^k, against housing pressure for housing type k, L_i^k, and housing provision for housing type k, H_i^k. House price for housing type k, h_i^k, does not appear on the right-hand side of the BLV dynamics equations but has a significant effect on housing pressure, and will clearly affect different income groups in different ways. One of the phenomena that might be better understood through this analysis is gentrification, and house price is clearly an important factor in this. In order to plot a graph for a single iteration with a range of house prices for one zone, some simplifying assumptions need to be made. For a graph produced for zone i, it is assumed that:

1 employment is static in zone i;
2 in zone i, housing provision for housing type k, H_i^k, is static;
3 service accessibility is static throughout the region; and
4 house prices in zones other than i are static.

The second of these assumptions is reasonable in most cases because housing provision evolves much more slowly than house price.

To demonstrate these ideas, an example residential zone graph is plotted in Figure 4.10a for zone 141 (near Doncaster) on iteration 200 of a model run using the best-fit model parameters. Figure 4.10b displays the housing pressure for each income group. The curve for each income group is fairly wide because the θ^w parameter is small[3] ($\theta^w = 0.000001$). This parameter controls the impact of monetary travel cost and house price on journey to work decisions for each income group. Each income group will have a preferred house price that is dependent on

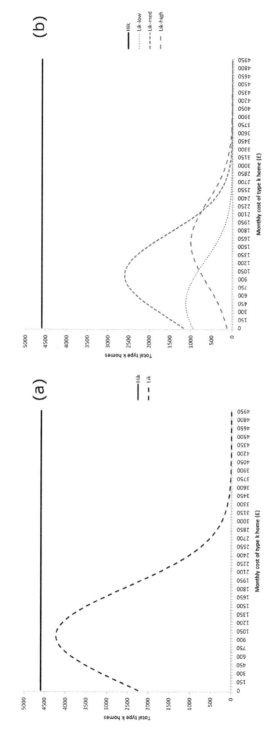

Figure 4.10 Residential zone graph for zone 141 (near Doncaster) on iteration 200, with $\theta^{w} = 0.000001$ showing (a) overall housing pressure and (b) housing pressure by income group

their budget, and the lower the θ^w parameter, the wider the range of house prices each income group will accept around the preferred price.

Figure 4.11 shows the same graph plotted using a higher θ^w parameter (θ^w = 0.0001). The peak(s) for each income group in Figure 4.11b are narrower, and this produces a number of stable intersections between the housing pressure and housing provision lines. The housing pressure curve for each income group can have multiple peaks if there are multiple zones to which commuters living in this zone will travel to (because monetary travel costs impact housing budget). The provision of type k housing, H_i^k, also determines the number of intersections. In Figure 4.10, there are no intersections, while in Figure 4.11 there are three. Only the rightmost intersection on each peak is stable due to the way the dynamics work. If the shape or position of the lines plotted in the graph changes, new stable intersections can appear or existing stable intersections can disappear, causing the current house price in a zone to shift from one income group's preference to another. This can then bring about a change in the demographic that occupies a particular zone.

In order to better understand the evolution of the residential system in a particular zone, many zone graphs can be plotted back to back in order to build a surface that covers several hundred iterations. Figure 4.12 shows the first 300 iterations of a model run. Figure 4.12a shows how the housing pressure for housing type k, L_i^k, changes shape, while the housing provision for housing type k, H_i^k, stays fairly stable. Figure 4.12b displays how the actual house price is affected by the change in the shape of the housing pressure for housing type k, L_i^k, surface. Early on in the model run, the stable intersections near the preferred house price for low- and medium-income groups disappear, and so the house price jumps to the preferred house price for the high-income group. As a result, the population in the zone changes from the low- to high-income band. This demonstrates how gentrification can be reproduced by a model of this kind. The model here contains two kinds of housing: small and large. The starting house price for each type is different so it would be possible to end up with different house prices for each type at equilibrium – a demonstration of the influence of path dependence.

4.5 Concluding comments

We have developed a comprehensive dynamic urban model of the evolution of multiple urban subsystems that has its roots in the Lowry model and introduces dynamics into that model. It featured BLV-type dynamics for two types of unregulated services, as well as housing provision and house prices. The model was tested by applying it to the metropolitan county of South Yorkshire. A results grid was generated to identify discontinuities across the many subsystems represented in this model. Single and multiple zone discontinuities were found in many of the subsystems. An example of gentrification occurring in one zone was analysed using a residential zone graph. This graph provided an explanation for how and why changes in the mix of income groups in a zone occur based on house price, housing provision and housing pressure.

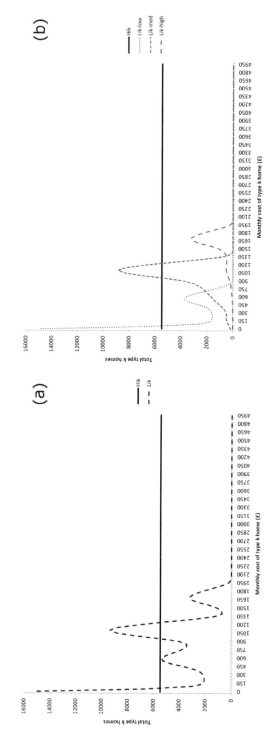

Figure 4.11 Residential zone graph for zone 141 (near Doncaster) on iteration 200, with $\theta^w = 0.0001$ showing (a) overall housing pressure and (b) housing pressure by income group

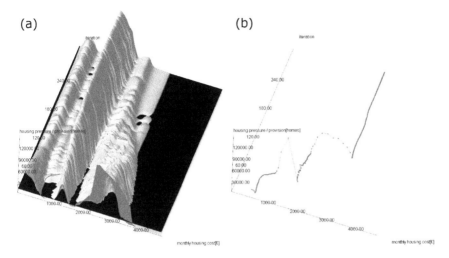

Figure 4.12 Residential zone graph evolution over 300 iterations: (a) housing
pressure and housing provision surfaces, and (b) actual zone
house price

An interactive visual simulation of this kind of model is helpful for understanding path dependence, emergent self-organisation and discontinuities. The
interactive visual interface provided a large number of simultaneous viewpoints
on the evolution of the simulated system and allowed repeated playback of its
evolution. This allowed detailed exploration of the dynamics in many subsystems.
Development and use of such a large dynamic model would have been much more
difficult without this kind of interface.

One problem identified during model testing is that the zone system used in
this model is possibly too coarse – a finer grid might capture more detail between
the centre and periphery of each particular city, for example. However, more zones
would require more computing power and may impact on being able to run the
model quickly and interactively on a desktop computer. This is clearly something
that could be improved upon in future.

Appendix 4.1 Specification of variables

Table 4.1 Exogenous model variables

Symbol	Description
T	The number of zones in the system
V_i	Total land in zone i
S^k	Attractiveness multiplier for type k housing
α	Impact of service centre size on service trip decisions

continued . . .

Table 4.1 Continued

Symbol	Description
ε^x	Speed of response of type x services to profit signals
ψ_1	Rate at which house prices respond to changes in the system
ψ_2	Rate at which housing provision responds to changes in the system
θ^w	Impact of monetary travel cost and house price on residential location/ journey to work decisions for type w people
a^x	Area per service industry x employee
σ	Inverse activity rate
e^{xw}	Average expenditure of type w people on type x services
y^{wx}	Proportion of type x service jobs that provide income level w
y^{wB}	Proportion of basic jobs that provide income level w
q^w	Proportion of budget spent on housing (after subtracting travel to work costs) by type w people
E_j^{Bw}	Total basic employment in zone j for type w people
μ^w	Impact of travel cost on service usage decisions for type w people
β^w	Impact of non-monetary travel cost on residential location/journey to work decisions for type w people
c_{ij}	Travel cost from zone i to zone j
c'_{ij}	Monetary travel cost from zone i to zone j
s	Monetary cost of journey to work per km per month (converts c_{ij} into c'_{ij})
ω^w	Total budget for type w people
ξ^{t1}	Proportion of population who change job and home every time-step
ξ^{t2}	Proportion of population who change job only every time-step
ξ^{t3}	Proportion of population who change home only every time-step
ξ^{t4}	Proportion of population who stay unchanged every time-step

Table 4.2 Endogenous model variables – part 1

Symbol	Description
K_i^x	Rent costs for one unit area of service x in zone i
N_i	Land used in zone i before constraints applied
G	Required growth rate for basic industry
G'	Growth rate for basic industry adjusted for land constraints
Y_i	Normalising factor for constraining land use in zone i
P_i	Current population of workers in zone i
P_i^w	Population of type w workers in zone i
E_j	Total employment in zone j
E_j^B	Total basic employment in zone j
E_j^{Bw}	Total basic employment in zone j that provides income level w
E_j^w	Total employment in zone j that provides income level w
E_j^x	Total service x employment in zone j
E_j^{xw}	Total service x employment in zone j that provides income level w
E_j^{uw}	The number of type w job-seekers in zone j
h_i^k	Type k house price for zone i
H_i^k	Number of type k homes in zone i
$H_i^{k'}$	Number of vacant type k homes in zone i

continued . . .

Table 4.2 Continued

Symbol	Description
H_i^{k2}	Number of type k homes in zone i that are fixed by people with type 2 location behaviour (job movers)
H_i^{k4}	Number of type k homes in zone i that are fixed by people with type 4 location behaviour (non-movers)
$E_j^{w'}$	Number of vacant type w jobs in zone j
E_j^{w3}	Number of type w jobs in zone j that are fixed by people with type 3 location behaviour (home movers)
E_j^{w4}	Number of type w jobs in zone j that are fixed by people with type 4 location behaviour (non-movers)

Table 4.3 Endogenous model variables – part 2

Symbol	Description
L_i^k	Total number of residents wanting to live in an ideal hypothetical type k home in zone i
U_{ij}^{kw}	Number of residents with income w wanting to live in their ideal hypothetical type k home in zone i and work in zone j
T_{ij}^{kwn}	Number of householders with income w living in type k housing in zone i and working in zone j with location behaviour n
S_{ij}^{xw}	Total spending by type w people living in zone i on type x services in zone j
D_j^x	Total service x expenditure in zone j
Z_i^w	Combined accessibility of all service types for residents in zone i with income w
Z_i^{wx}	Accessibility of type x services for residents in zone i with income w
W_j^x	Total service x provision in zone j
O_i^{wk}	Percentage of type k houses in zone i currently occupied by type w people
E	Total system employment
H	Total number of homes in the system
S	The difference between total real employment and total real housing capacity
Q_i^w	Total population of type w workers and non-workers in zone i
F	Total real employment (excluding jobseekers)
J	Total real housing provision (excluding temporary homes)

Table 4.4 Variable indices

Symbol	Description
W^x	Service type
$W_{i,j,m}$	Zone
W^w	Person income band
W^k	Housing type
W^n	Mover pool

Appendix 4.2 The dynamic model

A4.2.1 Basic industry

A basic employment growth rate is set for each time-step (uniform across the region). If this causes the land constraints in a zone to be exceeded, then the total amount of basic industry is constrained in that zone and the 'surplus' growth is redistributed. The detailed mechanism is in Dearden (2012). This process generates $\{E_i^B\}$.

A4.2.2 Regulated service industry sub-model

The evolution of regulated services, such as health and education, is often planned rather than determined in a market. Here, a simple assumption is made that a given initial service provision will grow proportionately with changes in the regional population. The growth rate matches the last percentage change in the system population. Then a similar mechanism is used to constrain land use as was described for basic employment. Alternatively, these variables can be set exogenously to represent planned change.

This process generates $\{W_j^x\}$ and $\{E_i^x\}$ for services x that are regulated.

A4.2.3 Unregulated service industry sub-model

The unregulated – retail and other consumer driven – services are represented using the standard BLV retail model framework. For each of these, in turn, the following steps are run through. First, the rent for unregulated services x in each zone K_j^x is calculated based on the accessibility to population (workers and non-workers) scaled by a constant γ and to the power of a constant ψ:

$$K_j^x = \gamma \left(\sum_i \sum_w Q_i^w \, \exp\left(-\mu^w c_{ij}\right) \right)^{\psi} \tag{4.17}$$

Service usage trips S_{ij}^{xw} are calculated between each pair of zones for each person type:

$$S_{ij}^{xw} = \frac{e^{xw} Q_i^w \left(W_j^x\right)^{\alpha} \exp\left(-\mu^w c_{ij}\right)}{\sum_m \left(W_m\right)^{\alpha} \exp\left(-\mu^w c_{im}\right)} \tag{4.18}$$

An inverse activity rate is used to include demand from non-workers in these calculations.

The key step is now to introduce explicit dynamics. Total service revenue D_j^x (Equation 4.19) attracted to each zone and unit area costs K_j^x are used to calculate the change in unregulated service provision ΔW_j^x:

$$D_j^x = \sum_{iw} S_{ij}^{xw} \tag{4.19}$$

$$\Delta W_j^x = \varepsilon^x \left(D_j^x - K_j^x W_j^x \right) \tag{4.20}$$

The term in brackets is the level of profit for the service in the zone. If these changes cause the land constraints in a zone to be exceeded, then the total land used by the unregulated service industries is constrained in that zone. This process generates $\{W_j^x\}$ for unregulated services x. An updated level of unregulated service employment can then be calculated:

$$E_j^x = \frac{W_j^x}{a^x} \tag{4.21}$$

A4.2.4 Residential location sub-model

The residential location sub-model is the most complex of the sub-models. It is disaggregated by three home types (small, large and temporary) and three resident income groups (low, medium and high).

First, change in house price Δh_i^k is calculated based on the difference between the housing provision H_i^k and housing pressure L_i^k (which is calculated at a later stage below – see Equation 4.37):

$$\Delta h_i^k = \varphi_1 \left[L_i^k - H_i^k \right] \tag{4.22}$$

$$\Delta h_i^{\text{temporary}} = 0 \tag{4.23}$$

In the first time-step, it is assumed that housing pressure is equal to housing provision so there is no change. In later time-steps, the housing pressure calculated in the previous time-step is used. As we will see, we need to construct temporary housing (described later) as part of a mechanism to balance available jobs and available homes. The 'price' of temporary housing is assumed to be static $\delta h_i^{\text{temporary}}$ (Equation 4.23). A similar system is used to calculate change in housing provision H_i^k on a fully dynamic basis:

$$\Delta H_i^k = \varphi_2 \left[L_i^k - H_i^k \right] \tag{4.24}$$

$$\Delta H_i^{\text{temporary}} = 0 \tag{4.25}$$

Since house prices usually change more quickly than housing provision, ψ_1 is set greater than ψ_2. Both these mechanisms are from Wilson (1974). The same land constraint mechanism as described in the other sub-models is used, so if these changes cause the land constraints in a zone to be exceeded, then the total land used by housing in that zone is constrained. Temporary housing is excluded from this process since it is assumed to take up no land.

Next, total employment in each zone is disaggregated by income group, w:

$$E_j^w = y^{wB} E_j^B + \sum_x y^{wx} E_j^x \tag{4.26}$$

A requirement of the journey to work model (described later) is that the number of jobs and homes in the region is balanced. To do this, total real employment F and total real housing provision J are calculated. Then a supply of either jobseeker provision[4] E_i^{ww} to make up a shortfall of employment (Equation 4.29) or temporary homes H_i^{temp} (representing mainly long-distance commuting from outside the region) to make up a shortfall of housing is provided:

$$F = \sum_i \left(E_j^B + \sum_x E_j^x \right) \tag{4.27}$$

$$J = \sum_i \sum_{k \neq \text{temp}} H_i^k \tag{4.28}$$

$$S = F - J \tag{4.29}$$

$$E_i^{uw} = \begin{cases} 0, & S \geq 0 \\ \text{otherwise,} & \left| S\left(\dfrac{F_i}{F} \right) \right| \end{cases} \tag{4.30}$$

$$H_i^{temp} = \begin{cases} 0, & S \leq 0 \\ \text{otherwise,} & \dfrac{S}{T} \end{cases} \tag{4.31}$$

where T is the number of zones in the system, F_i is total real employment in zone i and S is the shortfall of either homes (if positive) or jobs (if negative).

Combined accessibility to services Z_i^w is used as a simple representation of the residential attractiveness of a particular zone. This is calculated and used in an employment-constrained journey to work model U_{ij}^{kw} to calculate housing pressure L_i^k. This gives us a measure of where residents would ideally live and work if there were no constraints on housing provision. Temporary housing is excluded from these calculations to ensure that 'real' housing is constructed to make up any shortfall (we assume that long-distance commuters will eventually move into the region permanently). An additional multiplier S^k is included to differentiate between the attractiveness of different kinds of housing, in this case small versus large:

$$Z_i^w = \prod_x \sum_j \left(W_j^x \right)^\alpha \exp\left(-\mu^w c_{ij} \right) \tag{4.32}$$

$$U_{ij}^{kw} = C_j^w E_j^w S^k Z_i^w \exp\left(-\beta^w c_{ij}\right) \exp\left(-\phi^w \left[h_i^k - q^w \left(w - c_{ij}'\right)\right]^2\right) \qquad (4.33)$$

$$C_j^w = \frac{1}{\sum_i \sum_k S^k Z_i^w \exp\left(-\beta^w c_{ij}\right) \exp\left(-\phi^w \left[h_i^k - q^w \left(w - c_{ij}'\right)\right]^2\right)} \qquad (4.34)$$

$$L_i^k = \sum_j \sum_w U_{ij}^{kw} \qquad (4.35)$$

$$L_i^{\text{temporary}} = 0 \qquad (4.36)$$

To calculate residential location, a spatial interaction model based on the one described by Wilson (1974: 187) is used. The version shown here differs in that disaggregation by householder status (head of household or not)[5] has been removed and feedback has been introduced into the model to allow the rate of change to be controlled by the relative sizes of the four mover pools in the model. The mover pools are defined as:

1   people changing home and employment;
2   people changing employment only;
3   people changing home only; and
4   people changing neither home or employment.

The mover pool sizes are represented by four parameters:

$$\xi^1 + \xi^2 + \xi^3 + \xi^4 = 1 \qquad (4.37)$$

These are used to calculate for every zone: the number of homes occupied by job movers H_i^{k2} and H_i^{kw2} and fixed residents H_i^{k4} and H_i^{kw4}, the number of homes on the market $H_i^{k'}$, the number of jobs occupied by home movers E_j^{w3} and fixed residents E_j^{w4}, and the number of vacant jobs $E_j^{w'}$:

$$H_i^{k2} = \xi^2 H_i^k \qquad (4.38)$$

$$H_{ij}^{kw2} = H_i^{k2} O_i^{wk} \qquad (4.39)$$

$$H_i^{k4} = \xi^4 H_i^k \qquad (4.40)$$

$$H_i^{kw4} = H_i^{k4} O_i^{wk} \qquad (4.41)$$

$$H_i^{k'} = H_i^k - \left(H_i^{k2} + H_i^{k4} \right) \tag{4.42}$$

$$E_j^{w3} = \xi^3 E_i^w \tag{4.43}$$

$$E_j^{w4} = \xi^4 E_i^w \tag{4.44}$$

$$E_j^{w'} = E_j^w - \left(E_j^{w3} + E_j^{w4} \right) \tag{4.45}$$

These totals are used to calculate the balancing factors for the journey to work equations. These balancing factors are calculated iteratively. Iterating 50 times through the entire set of balancing factors (each model time-step) allows calculation of flows that meet the constraints reasonably accurately. Journey to work trips T_{ij}^{kw1}, T_{ij}^{kw2}, T_{ij}^{kw3}, T_{ij}^{kw4} that are disaggregated by housing type k, income band w and mover pool n are calculated:

$$T_{ij}^{kw1} = K^1 A_i^{k11} B_j^{w1} H_i^{k'} E_j^{w'} \exp\left(-\beta^w c_{ij} \right) \exp\left(-\theta^w \left[h_i^k - q^w \left(w - c_{ij}' \right) \right]^2 \right) \tag{4.46}$$

$$T_{ij}^{kw2} = A_i^{k12} B_j^{w1} H_i^{kw2} E_j^{w'} \exp\left(-\beta^w c_{ij} \right) \tag{4.47}$$

$$T_{ij}^{kw3} = A_i^{k11} B_j^{w3} H_i^{k'} E_j^{w3} \exp\left(-\beta^w c_{ij} \right) \exp\left(-\theta^w \left[h_i^k - q^w \left(w - c_{ij}' \right) \right]^2 \right) \tag{4.48}$$

$$T_{ij}^{kw4} = A_i^{k14} B_j^{w4} H_i^{kw4} E_j^{w4} \exp\left(-\beta^w c_{ij} \right) \tag{4.49}$$

The balancing factors themselves are messy but straightforward. The explicit equations are given in Dearden (2012).

These flows are aggregated to calculate the new population of workers in each zone, P_i^w, and the new population of workers and non-workers Q_i^w using the inverse activity rate σ:

$$P_i^w = \sum_j \sum_k \sum_n T_{ij}^{kwn} \tag{4.50}$$

$$Q_i^w = P_i^w \sigma \tag{4.51}$$

In order to provide feedback into the journey to work spatial interaction model, the proportion of each home type occupied by residents from each income level O_i^{wk} is calculated:

$$O_i^{wk} = \frac{\sum_n \sum_j T_{ij}^{kwn}}{\sum_{w'} \sum_n \sum_j T_{ij}^{kw'n}} \qquad (4.52)$$

Appendix 4.3 South Yorkshire model data sources

A list of the data sources used is shown in Table 4.5. Spatial data was converted to 212 × 3 km zones covering South Yorkshire by fragmenting, allocating an area-based proportion of any totals to each fragment and then re-aggregating to the 3 km zone system.

Table 4.5 South Yorkshire model data sources

Data	Source
Basic, retail and other consumer-driven services employment	http://cider.census.ac.uk/cider/wicid/query.php 1991 SWS Set C (inc. home-workers in intra-zonal flow)
Education employment	www.neighbourhood.statistics.gov.uk 2005
Average house price	www.neighbourhood.statistics.gov.uk Changes of ownership by dwelling price for 2009
Population by income level	Leeds University micro-simulation data
Health employment	Estimated from http://nhs.uk and www.neighbourhood.statistics.gov.uk data

Notes

1 The average number of workers per household for South Yorkshire is 1.19, and so is reasonably close to 1.
2 The slower-changing endogenous subsystems (small and large housing provision) are not shown because they are much the same across the whole grid.
3 For the purposes of generating this graph, all θ^w parameters are set to the same value.
4 An assumption is made that jobseekers remain in the same income band when unemployed and retain the same standard of living.
5 The average number of workers per household for South Yorkshire is 1.19, and so is reasonably close to 1.

References

Dearden, J. (2012) *Using Interactive Data Visualisation to Explore Dynamic Urban Models*, PhD Thesis, Centre for Advanced Spatial Analysis, University College London.

Dearden, J. and Wilson, A. G. (2011) 'A framework for exploring urban retail discontinuities', *Geographical Analysis*, 43: 172–87.

Lowry, I. S. (1964) *A Model of Metropolis*, Santa Monica, CA: Rand Corporation.

Wilson, A. G. (1974) *Urban and Regional Models in Geography and Planning*, London: Wiley.

5 BLV and agent-based models

5.1 Introduction

In this chapter, we explore the relationship between dynamic entropy maximising models of spatial interaction and structure and agent-based models. The dynamics are added to spatial interaction models through a form of Lotka-Volterra equations, which, as we saw in Chapter 1, has led to these models being designated as BLV – Boltzmann-Lotka-Volterra – models. These models have a long history. ABMs – agent-based models – are more recent, based on agents that have 'development rules'. There is sometimes a confusion with CA (cellular automaton) models in which the cells are given development rules and so in some ways can seem like agents. This is resolved by Epstein and Axtell (1996) by distinguishing agents from an 'environment' (which can be a grid of cells). Here, we want to explore whether it is possible to define a set of agents, an environment and associated rules in such a way that there is an ABM model that is equivalent to any BLV model. If this can be established, then, since BLV models are typically more highly developed and realistic, this should point the way to building more realistic ABMs. We proceed as follows. We take the retail model as an archetypal BLV model and then seek to formulate an equivalent – or near-equivalent – ABM.

5.2 The retail model as an archetypal BLV model

We start with the usual model and then show how to convert it into an agent-based model, which will then allow us to compare the results of the two approaches. The usual retail equations are repeated here for convenience but with the definitions of earlier chapters:

$$S_{ij} = A_i e_i P_i W_j^\alpha \exp\left(-\beta c_{ij}\right) \tag{5.1}$$

where:

$$A_i = \frac{1}{\sum_k W_k^\alpha \exp\left(-\beta c_{ik}\right)} \tag{5.2}$$

to ensure that:

$$\sum_j S_{ij} = e_i P_i \tag{5.3}$$

and:

$$\sum_{ij} S_{ij} \log W_j = X \tag{5.4}$$

$\log W_j$ is taken as the measure of consumer benefits and X an estimate of the total benefits achieved.

Note that W_j^α can be written:

$$W_j^\alpha = \exp\left(\alpha \log W_j\right) \tag{5.5}$$

so that:

$$u_{ij} = \alpha \log W_j - \beta c_{ij} \tag{5.6}$$

can be taken as a measure of utility.

The usual hypothesis for representing the dynamics is:

$$\frac{dW_j}{dt} = \varepsilon\left(D_j - KW_j\right)W_j \tag{5.7}$$

where K is a constant such that KW_j can be taken as the (notional) cost of running the shopping centre in j. This equation then says that if the centre is profitable, it grows; if not, it declines. The parameter ε determines the speed of response to these signals. The equations 5.7 are forms of Lotka-Volterra equations, and hence the characterisation of these models as BLV models (Wilson 2008).

5.3 An agent-based retail model

We define two kinds of agents:

- Consumers (C), with retail expenditure; and
- Retailers (R), each running a single shop.[1]

Each consumer and retail agent can be located at a unique point in our region of interest, rather than being aggregated into zones. We then need to define an associated set of running costs for each R-agent and a matrix of interaction costs.

The C-agents will each be given a residential location, i – possibilities of changing these would involve a model extension. Each R-agent will seek a possible shop location, j. The i's and j's are now nodes in the environment. In one time period, the consumers will each deploy a utility maximisation rule –

on a probabilistic basis – to find a shop – the utility being given in Equation 5.6 as $u_{ij} = \alpha \log W_j - \beta c_{ij}$. Note that this involves 'looking' further than neighbouring cells in the environment, and hence mimics – in fact, generalises – Epstein and Axtell's 'vision' mechanisms in their 'sugarscape' model (Epstein and Axtell 1996). (This also has a relationship to Potts' models in the statistical mechanics of crystal lattices in which interactions extend beyond nearest neighbours.) At each j, the retailer will be able to sum the inflows and decide whether the revenue exceeds the costs or not (cf. Equation 5.7). In our trial ABM model, there will be a probability that a loss-making retailer will seek to relocate. In the terminology of Holland (1995), each agent has a stimulus and a response – consumers having income as the stimulus and spending it as a response, each retailer having the total revenue inflow as a stimulus and the possibility of relocation as a response. The retailer totalling inflows is equivalent to Holland's 'tagging' of (C) agents as a means of aggregating. The decision to relocate is an (R) agent interaction with the environment. We expect that running a model of this type would generate emergent behaviour as in the BLV model, and we put this to the test below.

The model to be tested works as follows. Each retailer calculates a *range of choice* factor R_j for its current shop location j by counting the number of other shops within n metres of itself, where n is, say, easy walking distance to other shops nearby – here, we use $n = 200$ m. We will refer to this range as the *range of choice distance*. R_j then represents the number of other shops a consumer would also be able to visit if it travelled to shop j. The value of R_j is recalculated every iteration of the model.

Each retailer calculates the net income f_j for their shop j every iteration:

$$f_j = D_j - K \qquad (5.8)$$

where D_j is the total income of shop j and K its operating costs. The total operating costs of all shops in the region are set equal to the total spending money of all consumers in the region. As a result, some shops will always be unprofitable, and as a result their owners will be looking to relocate.

At each iteration, a proportion of randomly chosen retailers are allowed to relocate. Only those retailers making no money ($f_j \leq 0$) will consider relocating when prompted. A retailer that decides to relocate has an equal chance of either moving to a random position in the region or moving near to one of its competitors. If it decides to move near a competitor, it will evaluate the profit made by every other shop k and use this to calculate a probability m_{jk} of moving near that shop:

$$m_{jk} = \frac{t_k}{\sum_l t_l} \qquad (5.9)$$

where t_k is the profit made by shop k. If a shop k is making a loss, then $t_k = 0$ and there will be no chance of another retailer relocating near it. Here, we define 'moving near to a competitor' as: moving to a random position that is at most n metres away from it, where n = *range of choice distance*.

A consumer's position in the region is fixed and represents the position of its home. Each consumer calculates the probability p_{ij} that it will travel from its home i to visit shop j:

$$p_{ij} = \frac{R_j^\alpha \exp\left(-\beta c_{ij}\right)}{\sum_k R_k^\alpha \exp\left(-\beta c_{ik}\right)} \tag{5.10}$$

As with the entropy maximising model, α represents the impact of range of choice on shopping decisions, β the impact of travel cost and c_{ij} is the travel cost between house i and shop j. The set of all p_{ij} for one consumer agent i makes up a probability distribution that represents the likelihood of that consumer shopping at each shop in the region. Each time a consumer is prompted to go shopping, it generates a uniform random number to choose a shop based on these probabilities. Each consumer agent has a fixed amount of money to spend when it goes shopping, and it always spends the full amount in its chosen shop. This amount can obviously vary across agents depending on the data used to initialise the model.

During the course of a model run, several retailers may locate within each other's *range of choice distance* and so mutually benefit each other by increasing each other's range of choice factor, R_j. We can think of a group of retailers that does this as making up an 'emergent' retail zone, which could, in practice, represent a row of shops, a high street or a shopping mall. Some pairs of retailers in the retail zone might be outside each other's *range of choice distance* and so not mutually benefit each other, but still be part of the same group because they are linked indirectly via other retailers. We can identify these groups as they form in the model using a recursive algorithm to identify closed groups of retailers that are all directly or indirectly connected to each other. The full algorithm is given in Appendix 5.1. The number of retailers in each emergent retail zone can be thought of as equivalent to the W_j term in the entropy maximising model and the value of R_j for each retailer in the centre may be less than or equal to this term depending on its layout. An alternative measure of attractiveness for a retailer could use the W_j term for the retail zone it belongs to rather than the R_j term. The formula for p_{ij} would then be:

$$p_{ij} = \frac{W_j^\alpha \exp\left(-\beta c_{ij}\right)}{\sum_k W_k^\alpha \exp\left(-\beta c_{ik}\right)} \tag{5.11}$$

One iteration of the model comprises the following steps:

1   Each consumer chooses a shop and spends all their money there.
2   All retailers calculate their profit level.
3   ε per cent of retailers are given the option of relocating.
4   All retailers recalculate their range of choice factor, R_j (because one retailer moving can affect multiple neighbours).

5   The size of each emergent retail zone is calculated.
6   All consumers recalculate their set of probabilities p_{ij}.

The percentage ε represents the rate at which retailers respond to profit levels and so performs a similar role to ε in the entropy maximising model.

5.4 Results: a comparison

5.4.1 System overview

In order to properly test the agent-based model, we choose to model the metropolitan county of South Yorkshire in the UK. By modelling a real system, we are better able to judge whether the outputs are realistic or not. Full details of data sources and how we use them to initialise each model are given in Appendix 5.2. Figure 5.1 shows the raw data plotted on a map and gives an idea of the distribution of retail outlets within the county (repeated here from Chapters 2 and 3 for convenience).

5.4.2 System equilibrium

The BLV model generally tends towards an equilibrium solution. We can detect this by examining the change in size of each retail zone, W_j. Here, we define equilibrium as less than 0.01 per cent change in the size of each retail zone for at least 250 iterations. We abandon a model run after 100,000 iterations in case the model does not converge.

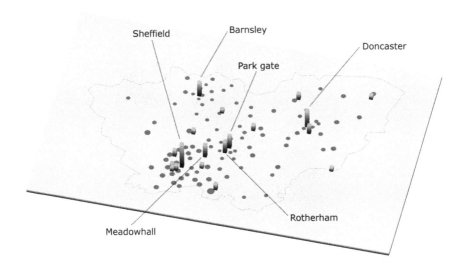

Figure 5.1 Visualisation of the South Yorkshire data

For the agent-based model, detecting equilibrium is more difficult because whatever structure emerges is not fixed. For this purpose, we use the fuzzy numerical technique developed by Hagen-Zanker *et al.* (2006) for comparing continuous raster maps. At 100 iteration intervals, we calculate the number of retailers in each cell of a 40 × 40 grid that covers the region. We use the fuzzy numerical similarity metric to compare consecutive grids,[2] and if this metric exceeds 0.996 (a threshold found by experimentation) we assume that the model has reached a stable state.

The rate of response parameters in each model were set as follows: for the BLV model, we use $\varepsilon = 0.003$, and for the ABM, we set $\varepsilon = 1\%$.

5.4.3 Emergent structures

Our first job is to see what kind of structures and behaviour, if any, emerge from the agent-based model. For this, we use population data for South Yorkshire to generate consumer agents inside Census Area Statistics (CAS) ward boundaries (Figure 5.2) but start with a uniform random distribution of retailers across the region. For this first exploration, we choose the model parameters $\alpha = 1.0$, $\beta = 0.5$. The output using Equation 5.10 is shown in Figure 5.3 and the output using Equation 5.11 is shown in Figure 5.4.

In both cases, realistic structures emerge with large clusters of retailers appearing at the major cities/towns in the region: Sheffield, Barnsley, Rotherham and Doncaster. Equation 5.10 appears to produce more compact retail centres than Equation 5.11, presumably because there is more benefit in locating close to as many other retailers as possible.

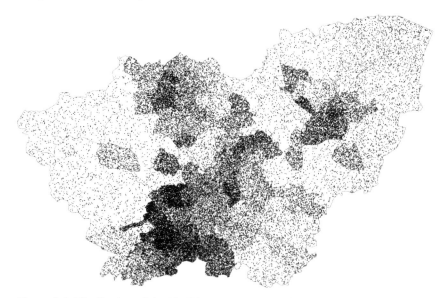

Figure 5.2 Distribution of the 52,722 consumer agents in the South Yorkshire model generated from CAS wards

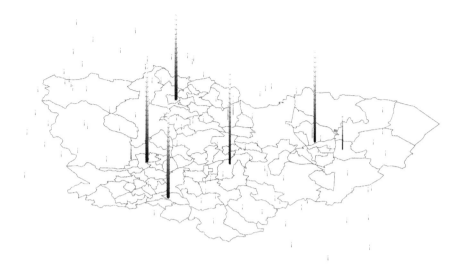

Figure 5.3 Structure in the model using Equation 5.10 (shop height ∝ number of other shops nearby)

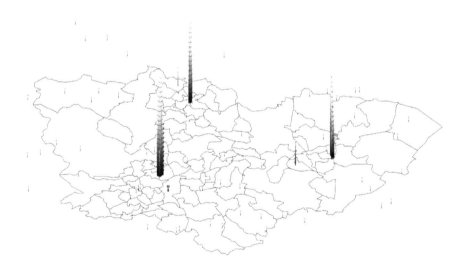

Figure 5.4 Structure in the model using Equation 5.11 (shop height ∝ number of other shops nearby)

5.4.4 Results grids

For the BLV model, a results grid can be plotted as in earlier chapters, and this shows the possibilities of emergent behaviour and of phase changes through plots of the order parameter. The results grid in Figure 5.5 represents the parameter space formed by varying the parameters $\alpha = 0.2$ to 2.0 and $\beta = 0.2$ to 2.0, using a step size in both cases of 0.2.

Figure 5.6 shows a surface plot of the order parameter $N(W_j > 300,000)$ for the same parameter space as Figure 5.5.

For comparison, we produce a results grid for both variants of the agent-based model and show the results in Figures 5.7 and 5.8. A visual comparison of the grids suggests that both models are producing similar outputs with the BLV model grid in Figure 5.5.

Plots of the order parameter $N(W_j > 300,000)$ in Figures 5.9 and 5.10 indicate that the behaviour of the agent-based model is largely similar to the BLV model across the parameter space; however, there are some clear differences, especially when Equation 5.10 is used. This may be, in part, because the agent-based model is a much more noisy system than the BLV model.

5.4.5 Model calibration

We can measure the goodness of fit of each of the model runs in the results grids above to find a best fit for each model.

The goodness of fit of the output from the BLV model is easily checked against data using the coefficient of determination, R-squared, because we have a fixed zone system – each retail zone in the model is at the same position as its equivalent zone in the data. We find the best fit at ($\alpha = 1.0932191948797$, $\beta = 0.5260256949075$), which produces an R-squared value of 0.8. The output

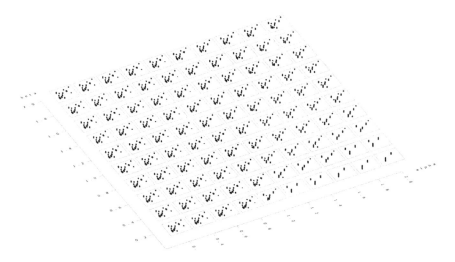

Figure 5.5 Results grid for the BLV model in (α, β) space (retail zone height $\propto$ floor space)

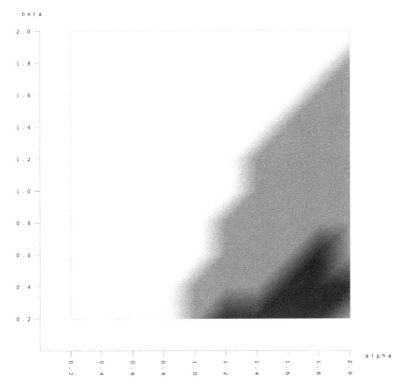

Figure 5.6 Order parameter surface plot for the BLV model in (α, β) space; colour scale indicates number of retail centres greater than 300,000 m² where white = 0 and black = 2

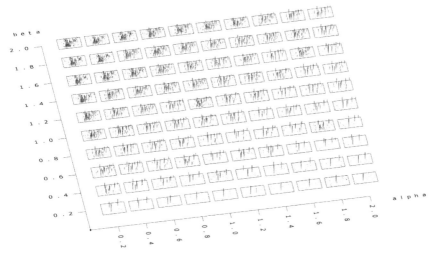

Figure 5.7 Results grid in (α, β) space for the agent-based model using Equation 5.10 (shop height $\propto$ number of other shops nearby)

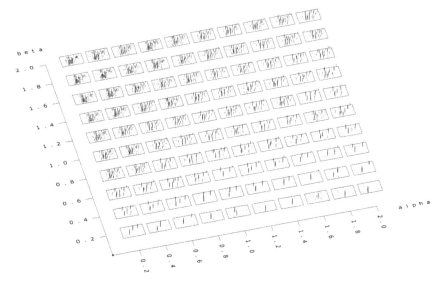

Figure 5.8 Results grid in (α, β) space for the agent-based model using Equation 5.11 (shop height ∝ number of other shops nearby)

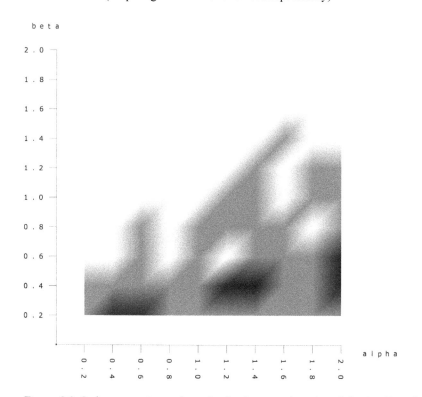

Figure 5.9 Order parameter surface plot for the agent-based model using Equation 5.10 in (α, β) space; colour scale indicates number of retail centres greater than 300,000 m² where white = 0 and black = 2

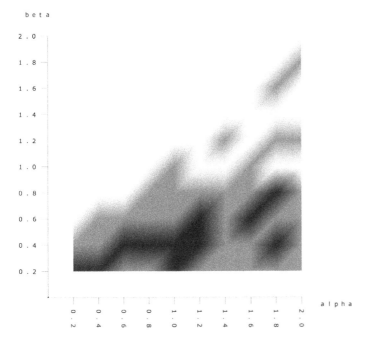

Figure 5.10 Order parameter surface plot for the agent-based model using Equation 5.11 in (α, β) space; colour scale indicates number of retail centres greater than 300,000 m^2 where white = 0 and black = 2

Figure 5.11 Best-fit BLV model run for South Yorkshire; retail zones are shown by blocks (height $\propto$ floor space) and residential zones are shown by circles (radius $\propto$ spending power)

(Figure 5.11) matches the real system reasonably well, however, because we are not taking into account the complexities of the transport network in our measure of distance, we are missing some retail zones, most notably the large Meadowhall shopping centre near Sheffield.

Measuring the output from the agent-based model is more difficult because retail zones can emerge anywhere on the map. We again make use of the fuzzy numerical comparison technique because it allows us to compare two retail systems that differ in both position and number of centres. To do this, we convert both the town centres data (see Appendix 5.2) and the agent-based model output to a raster grid. We find the best-fit parameter set for Equation 5.10 at ($\alpha = 1.57$, $\beta = 1.15$) (Figure 5.12) and for Equation 5.11 at ($\alpha = 1.57$, $\beta = 0.73$) (Figure 5.13).

5.5 Conclusion

We have demonstrated a zoneless agent-based model of urban retail in which retail centres emerge due to individual retailers locating near each other. By comparing the outputs across a portion of (α, β) parameter space, we have demonstrated that it produces similar results to the well-established BLV urban retail model. This work is a first step towards defining an agent-based model that is equivalent to any BLV model.

In comparing the models side by side, it becomes clear that the BLV model is far less computationally intensive to run when dealing with very large systems. For example, the real population of South Yorkshire is approximately 1.2 million people; however, in order to produce fast run times, we modelled the region using ~50,000 consumer agents and ~500 retailer agents (see Appendix 5.2 for more details). Given more time and/or computing power, the number of retailer and consumer agents could be increased closer to the real number.

The agent-based model is potentially easier to disaggregate because we can quickly introduce multiple agent types through class-based inheritance in an object-oriented programming language.

Here, we used macro-level data to both initialise the agent-based model and calibrate its output. It would be preferable to use micro-level data to generate and calibrate the retailer and consumer agents, though locating appropriate sources of data at this scale is difficult.

The next steps would involve more disaggregation – that is, more agent types – and then to extend the model in the direction of a comprehensive model that drew in a wider range of urban sub-models – possibly using the Lowry (1964) model as an archetype, but also moving towards realism (cf. Wilson 2006).

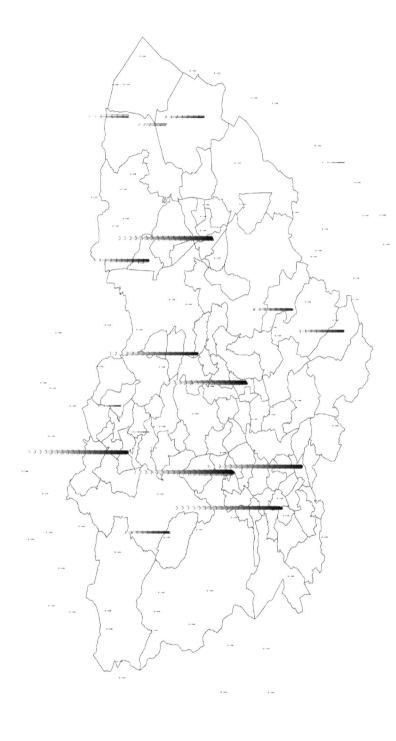

Figure 5.12 Best-fit model run using Equation 5.10 (shop height ∝ number of other shops nearby)

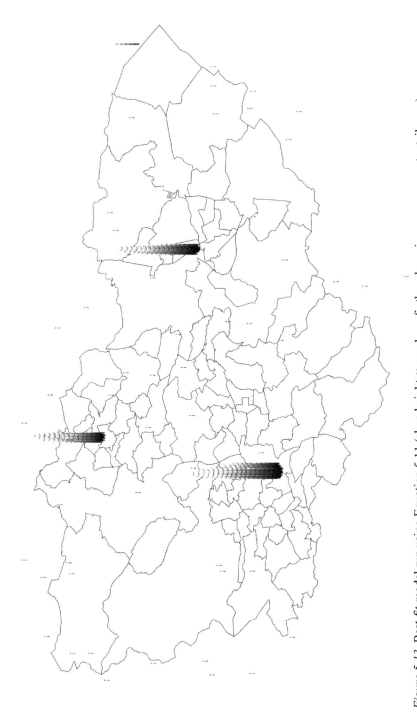

Figure 5.13 Best-fit model run using Equation 5.11 (shop height ∝ number of other shops in same emergent retail zone)

Appendix 5.1 An algorithm for calculating the boundary and membership of emergent retail zones

Pseudo-code is given here for calculating the emergent retail zones that appear in the model.

Setup an empty list of shops called processedList
    While there are still shops not in processedList
        Choose a shop s that is not in processedList
        Setup an empty list called shopList
        Call function **findClosedGroup** with s, shopList and processedList as parameters
        shopList now contains all the shops in one retail zone

The recursive function **findClosedGroup** does the following:

For each shop t nearby
    If t is not already in shopList
        Add t to shopList
        Add t to processedList
        Call function **findClosedGroup** with t, shopList and processedList as parameters

Appendix 5.2 Data sources

The retail data come from the Town Centres project 2004. We use the *total retail floor space* attribute from each town centre area to:

- *For the BLV model*: set the floor space of each retail zone in the BLV model.
- *For the ABM model*: determine the number of retailer agents we need to generate inside the town centre area for the ABM model. We do this by dividing the *total retail floor space* by an average shop size of ~2,800 m², which produced about 500 retailer agents for the region. The average shop size was chosen to reduce the computation load but could obviously be reduced given more time.

The population data are from the 2001 UK Census. We use the *All people* field from the KS001 Usual resident population table for the CAS Wards boundaries. Then:

- *For the BLV model*: the centroid of each CAS Ward is the location of each residential zone and the P_i value is set to the *All people* value.
- *For the ABM model*: the *All people* value, divided by an aggregation factor, decides the number of consumer agents we generate at random positions inside the CAS Ward boundary. In this case, the aggregation factor was set to 24 (meaning that each consumer agent represents 24 people) and produced

~50,000 consumer agents in the model. Again, this was done to allow for reasonable computation times.

Average retail spending per month data (derived from the ONS Family Spending 2010 Edition) was used to:

* *For the BLV model*: set the e_i value for each residential zone.
* *For the ABM model*: set the spending money available to each consumer agent.

For simplicity, all travel costs were calculated from the Euclidean distance between two points.

Notes

1   For simplicity, we are only modelling independent retailers. An interesting extension of the model might be to include chain stores with one retailer owning multiple shops.
2   We use a neighbourhood size of 10.

References

Epstein, J. M. and Axtell, R. (1996) *Growing Artificial Societies*, Cambridge, MA: MIT Press.

Hagen-Zanker, A., Engelen, G., Hurkens, J., Vanhout, R. and Uljee, I. (2006) *Map Comparison Kit 3: User Manual*, Maastricht: Research Institute for Knowledge Systems.

Holland, J. H. (1995) *Hidden Order: How Adaptation Builds Complexity*, Reading, MA: Addison Wesley.

Lowry, I. S. (1964) *A Model of Metropolis*, Memorandum RM.4035 - RC, Santa Monica, CA: Rand Corporation.

Wilson, A. G. (2006) 'A generalised representation for a comprehensive urban and regional model', *Computers, Environment and Urban Systems*, 31: 148–61.

Wilson, A. G. (2008) 'Boltzmann, Lotka and Volterra and spatial structural evolution: an integrated methodology for some dynamical systems', *Journal of the Royal Society, Interface*, 5: 865–71.

Wilson, A. G. and Oulton, M. (1983) 'The corner shop to supermarket transition in retailing: the beginnings of empirical evidence', *Environment and Planning A*, 15(2): 265–74.

6 Gaming with dynamic models

6.1 Introduction

With over half the world's population now living in urban areas (Martine 2007), it is becoming increasingly important to understand how cities evolve so that we can ensure that urban environments are sustainable and serve the needs of their populace. The evolution of cities is influenced both by the actions of planners working in the public sector and the self-organising processes that occur in a city without any central control, such as those of the private market and private individuals (Garvin 2001).

Understanding urban evolution is, however, a significant challenge. Cities are systems of organised complexity (Weaver 1948; Jacobs 1961). Large-scale behaviours and structures can emerge out of the micro-scale interactions of people but are not easy to understand or predict from individual actions (Mitchell 2009). The behaviour of each component is dependent on the behaviour of many others, making it difficult to analyse any one part in isolation (Allen and Sanglier 1981). Cities also contain non-linear relationships between different parts, which further complicates analysis. One resulting phenomenon is path dependence (Arthur 1988), which means that random events in the evolution of a system can have a great influence on its future state. Another is the potential for discontinuities to occur – where small changes to one part of a system have disproportionately large effects elsewhere.

A better understanding of the dynamic behaviour of cities would help planners to manage the self-organising processes at work in the system. It should be possible, for example, to develop one part of a region without causing decline in other areas.

Dynamic urban models can be brought to bear for studying the evolution of urban systems. Increases in available computing power have allowed more detail to be represented but means that the models are becoming complex – examples being agent-based models (Schelling 1969) and Boltzmann-Lotka-Volterra (BLV) models (Wilson 2008). Computer simulation is one way of analysing such models, and involves running computational models and exploring the outputs. Simulations provide a useful way of examining the underlying models and theory, identifying new and simple regularities, and generating new hypotheses (Hartmann 1996). A simulation of this kind typically produces large volumes of data and involves complex relationships, so we require good analytical tools in order to make progress. Batty *et al.* (2004) introduce the idea of visual modelling and identify three potential benefits: (1) it can provide a simplifying viewpoint on complicated systems; (2) it enables exploration and discovery; and (3) it allows engagement with non-scientific experts. Extending a visual modelling interface to allow the user to participate in the simulation to affect the outcome in some way appears to be a natural next step. To see why this might be beneficial, it is useful to look at the typical mode of use for urban models:

> The implicit objective in the conventional approach to modeling is to produce forecasts of the most likely consequences of some discrete proposal for someone other than the model-builder. What the recipient of the forecast learns is no more than the contents of the forecast. Nothing, or nothing much, is learnt about the way in which the city works or about the role which the proposed project might play in its evolution.
>
> (Macmillan 1996)

Additionally, given the already described complex, non-linear nature of urban systems, producing accurate forecasts in a conventional sense is impossible (but see Chapter 3). It may be helpful to put a greater emphasis on exploring the processes at work to try to gain a greater understanding of how the system behaves in a generally applicable way, rather than focusing on one simulation outcome.

One way of doing this might be to use participatory computer simulation, first developed in the context of classroom learning by Wilensky and Stroup (1999). In participatory simulations, human-controlled agents can provide a complex and accurate behavioural model to apply to the solution of any given objectives in the simulation (Cacciaguerra and Roffilli 2005). In this framework, an urban simulation model could, for example, enable stakeholders to participate in the evolution of a simulated urban system. The model is then open to feedback from participants who can suggest improvements and changes to bring the simulated system closer to the real system. In this mode of use, it might be helpful to see urban models as in constant evolution themselves in the face of repeated use, feedback and development. The Kolb (1984) learning cycle (Figure 6.1) used in experiential learning suggests that the capability to experiment with system behaviour could be of benefit to stakeholders learning about the likely behaviour of a system – even if that experience is gained in a virtual system rather than a real one.

We explore participatory urban simulation here by developing two prototype systems that allow human participation in a computer simulation of urban retail. Both systems are derived from the agent-based model in Chapter 5. We start in Section 6.2 by exploring different ways of structuring user participation. We define our template agent-based retail model in Section 6.3, derive a demonstrator system from it in Section 6.4 and a game in Section 6.5, and then conclude the chapter in Section 6.6.

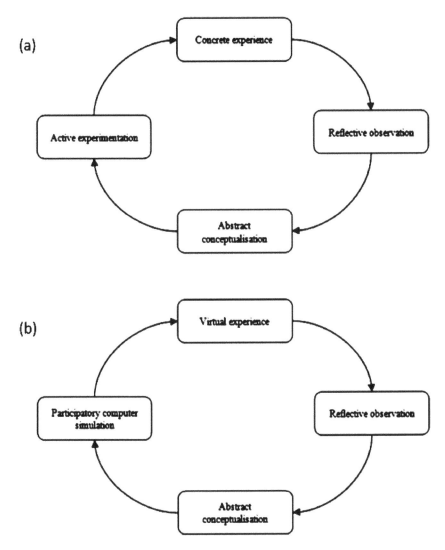

Figure 6.1 (a) Standard Kolb learning cycle and (b) participatory computer
 simulation learning cycle

6.2 Approaches for structuring user participation in simulations

Clearly, there are many different ways a user might participate in a simulated
system. In non-participatory urban simulations, the level of interaction is usually
restricted to adjusting exogenous model parameters in order to explore the range

of outputs. In a participatory simulation, we would expect more direct interaction with system entities. For example, Semboloni's (2007) online CityDev software uses a comprehensive agent-based model as the basis for a participatory simulation in which a human can generate new agents and control them. Its application to the development of a new suburb of Florence emphasises the role of private investors in determining the resulting urban structure. The type of underlying model will clearly play some part in determining what a user can and cannot do. Aggregate land use transportation models could, for example, allow a user to control different parts of the transport infrastructure or set planning policy in particular zones. In this chapter, we focus on agent-based models because they provide an opportunity for a user to control individual system actors. Participatory simulation has obvious similarities with serious games, which are rapidly gaining acceptance as an innovative and engaging way of teaching and learning in fields such as the military, government, education, corporate training and health care (Susi *et al.* 2007). There is a lot of overlap in the two areas, though clearly not every participatory simulation need involve gaming, and not every serious game need involve simulation; however, both involve participation in a process, and it is helpful to explore the two concepts together.

Many participatory simulations do not involve computers. One of the most well known is the paper-based beer game (Sterman 1989), which allows participants to learn about the behaviour of the retail supply chain. Reckien and Eisenack (2008) developed a non-computer role-playing game to teach participants about urban sprawl. The game was found to give participants a better understanding of the interdependencies between the different actors in the system, as well as familiarising them with the qualitative computer model that the simulation was based on. Barreteau *et al.* (2001) found benefits in applying a multi-agent system model alongside a non-computer role-playing simulation (derived from the model) for improving the management of irrigation systems in the Senegal River Valley. The role-playing game was found to make the computer model and its underlying assumptions more accessible to local stakeholders. It also helped to evaluate and validate the model. Similarly, Castella *et al.* (2005) used a role-playing game to collaboratively develop an agent-based model of agricultural dynamics with local stakeholders in Vietnam.

SimCity is the most well known computer game related to urban planning but was designed primarily for entertainment, and as a serious game fails in many areas (Lobo 2005), not least because the underlying model is hidden. Von Mammen and Jacob (2009) allow a player to control a computer simulation of swarming agents by adjusting the parameters that control the interaction of agents and by taking control of single agents, among other things. This kind of immersion is presented as a way of better understanding dynamic complex systems and so is obviously of relevance to cities. Van Bilsen *et al.* (2010) developed *SimPort-MV2*, a multiplayer computer game based around a planned extension to the port of Rotterdam. It was designed to give students and professionals the chance to explore different strategies for developing an international port while learning about the behaviour of complex adaptive systems. They present the view that simulation games are one of the only tools flexible enough for participants to learn about complex adaptive systems.

Here, we are interested in using participatory computer-based simulation to explore the process of urban evolution, focusing specifically on the phenomena already identified: interdependencies, self-organisation and emergence, discontinuities, and path dependence. To do this, we derive our prototype systems from an agent-based model that is known to demonstrate such phenomena. A participatory simulation derived from an agent-based model and structured as a game would provide each user with the opportunity to role-play subjectively as one of the agents in the simulation, competing with other agents, working within rules and constraints and eventually winning or losing, subject to some success criteria. The idea being that the user could gain insight into the important factors that determine the evolutionary path of an urban system, similar to the way human chess players develop expert knowledge about the important parts of the game, rather than using the brute force analysis applied by computer players. What form the game takes obviously depends on the roles available in the system being simulated. In the case of a retail system, the main agents are retailers, consumers, developers and the planning authority. It would be important to provide each player with a clear role and support multiple human players. For comparison purposes, we also develop a second form of participatory simulation structured as a demonstrator. With no criteria for success and no imposed rules (other than the constraints in the underlying model), this would provide a sandbox for objective experimentation with all elements of a system.

6.3 A simple retail agent-based model

The template for our participatory systems is the agent-based model developed in Chapter 5. Where the agent-based model runs automatically, with the computer updating all the entities in the simulation, the participatory systems only proceed once all participants have provided their input. By using an agent-based model, we are allowing exploration of a wide range of scales: from regional, through retail zone, right down to individual shops. The zone system in the model emerges from the behaviour of individual agents and is an example of second-order emergence (Squazzoni 2008) – macro-structures that emerge from micro-behaviour but then, in turn, influence that same micro-level behaviour.

One change over the original model is that if a retailer move would cause it to overlap with another shop, it is randomly displaced to a nearby, non-overlapping position – we assume all shopping zones are single storey. This is intended to help participants see more easily how many retailers exist in each retail zone.

For comparison with the participatory simulation systems, we first apply the agent-based model to the evolution of the metropolitan county of South Yorkshire. We use the best-fit parameters found for this model in Chapter 5 ($\alpha = 1.57$, $\beta = 0.73$). The model contains ~500 shops and ~50,000 households (due to constraints on time and computing power, some aggregation was necessary – each household agent represents ~24 real consumers). Figure 6.2 shows these agents located based on real data (see Appendix 5.2 of Chapter 5 for details of the data used). The initial conditions for the agent-based model differ in that the retailer agents are located in a uniform random way throughout the region.

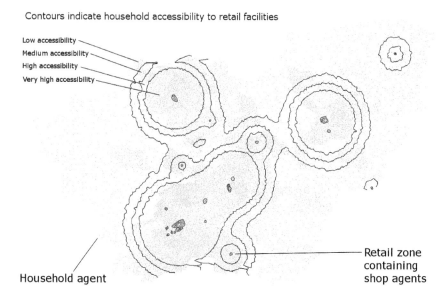

Figure 6.2 Household and retailer agent distribution derived from data

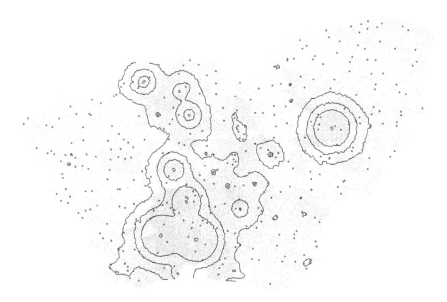

Figure 6.3 After 400 retailer moves (80 iterations) controlled by agent-based model

During the agent-based simulation run, one can see the process of retail zone emergence, growth and decline that occurs in the simulation. The retailers 'self-organise' into profitable clusters and disband unprofitable clusters. It is also apparent that retailers locate near where most households are. Path dependence is visible in the seeds of early randomly forming small clusters growing to form larger clusters at those points. We get some idea about interdependence in the reliance of retailers on one another to increase apparent consumer range of choice. After 400 retailer moves (which actually equates to 80 iterations with five shops moving every iteration), the ABM generates the system shown in Figure 6.3.

6.4 A demonstration retail system

We modify the retail ABM explained in Section 6.3 to construct a demonstrator in which the user can move the retailers in a region around without any obvious goals or structure. This mode allows exploration of interdependencies between entities at a range of scales (e.g. individual shops and retail zones). The immersive nature of the system means that the user can see what patterns are possible given the constraints of the model so that they might better understand the competition-driven self-organisation and emergence that appears in the agent-based model. This knowledge would hopefully then provide insights into the nature of real retail systems.

The user is given system-level metrics that could have an impact on the dynamics in the system: (1) the total proportion of retailers making a profit; and (2) the accessibility of households to retail facilities. The accessibility to retail facilities θ_i for householder i is defined as the combined attractiveness of all retailers from that location:

$$\theta_i = \sum_k W_k^\alpha \exp\left(-\beta c_{ik}\right) \tag{6.1}$$

Shop profitability is shown by the colour of each shop, red for unprofitable and green for profitable. The overall amount of profit made by all the shops in a retail zone is displayed over it as a text label. We manually calibrate values of accessibility through trial and error to fit into four categories: low, medium, high and very high, which is then used to visualise the accessibility to retail facilities for each household using contours. The user moves retailers by dragging and dropping them using the mouse. Multiple shops can be moved at the same time by dragging a selection box over them, making this relatively quick and easy. The state of the system updates every time the location of a retailer is changed. The stochastic nature of the model means that the system state will fluctuate over time – households can potentially change their shopping locations at every step, bringing the behaviour of the demonstration retail system closer to the uncertainty of the real world.

The demonstrator was tested using the exact same set-up as was described in the previous section. Using the demonstrator allows a participant to explore the impact of individual shops and entire retail zones on the rest of the retail system.

Retail zones form dynamically as retailers are moved around. As large retail zones form, individual retailers and small groups of shops nearby have little choice but to join the larger agglomeration to avoid being unprofitable. Path dependence is made clear by the fact that, with a limited number of moves, one can only achieve so much – moving a large retail zone is not really feasible if a high level of investment (in this case, in moves) has already been made. Use of the demonstrator suggests that the spatial form of a retail centre might be an important factor in its attractiveness to consumers. The Parkgate Shopping Park has an advantage over Rotherham because its purpose-built structure packs a similar number of shops into a smaller area and so offers visitors more convenient access, and it is probably seen as a more compact whole. It is certainly more attractive in our model. By contrast, Rotherham is made up of more spread out and separate streets, diluted by mixed uses. Parkgate has 118,000 m^2 of retail in an area of 125,000m^2 versus Rotherham's 105,000 m^2 spread out over 512,500m^2. A possible solution might be to increase the continuity and density of shops in Rotherham town centre. Rotherham town centre and many other high streets likely need updating in the face of competition from purpose-built shopping centres, something that is being tackled in Rotherham by the 25-year Rotherham Renaissance project.

6.5 A two-player urban retail game

We adapt the agent-based model into a game for two people to role-play as large chain-store retailers/developers, each owning half of all the shops in a region. This is not realistic but is offered on a simple proof-of-concept basis. The players compete to build the most profitable pattern of shops after a fixed number of shop moves. Writing a computer-controlled agent to represent this kind of large-scale organisation in a computer is complicated, so having a human play this role simplifies the system a great deal. To make the game fair, each player's group of shops is initially located in a near identical spatial pattern. This is done by allocating pairs of shops to random locations in the region and giving one shop to each player. There are no computer-controlled retailer agents. Each player takes it in turn to move a set number of shops, using a similar interface to that described for the demonstration retail system, after which the households in the region recalculate their shopping patterns. As with the demonstrator, each player has access to detailed information about the region: household density, the net income of each shop and retail accessibility level.

Figure 6.4 illustrates the end state after the retail game was played by two players for 40 turns, where each player moved five shops per turn. The game forces players to try to outdo their opponent, but it means more risky locations were tried. The winning player made better decisions about where to invest moves in terms of location and zone size. Low retail accessibility anywhere in the region was a useful signal to the players that a new centre might be built there, though this obviously depended on the carrying capacity of the location in terms of its overall spending power. In competition, it was difficult to not oversupply an area with retail facilities. Zones defined in inappropriate locations were likely to lose out in

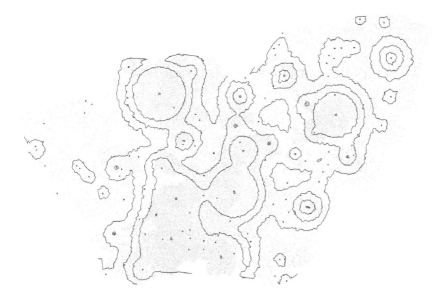

Figure 6.4 After 40 player turns each in the two-player game

competition with better-located zones. Discontinuities were observable at the retail zone scale when an existing retail zone became redundant in the eyes of consumers due to the appearance of a more attractive, usually larger or closer, retail zone.

6.6 Conclusions and future work

Human participation in simulations of complex urban systems has the potential to provide a useful and original point of view on the behaviour of dynamic urban models for the purposes of model development and improving our understanding of complex urban systems.

Participatory simulations of this kind could be used in teaching. They could also be used as an accessible and engaging way in to planning support systems (PSS) and might help to increase the currently low level of adoption in the planning community (Vonk *et al.* 2005). They have the capacity to make underlying models and data more transparent, make the complex non-linear dynamics of urban systems easier to understand and help planners become more familiar with the types of challenges they are likely to face under a range of different conditions when supporting a competitive market place. Where stakeholders are involved, participatory simulations could be helpful for informing and engaging with them about important issues.

The systems presented here are prototypes, but give some idea of what might be possible in future given more research in this area. These systems would likely need to be further developed with, and tested by, potential end users to ensure they match their requirements. Both systems provide useful but very different viewpoints on the processes at work in the simulation. They are potentially useful as hypothesis-generation tools and allow exploration of the interplay between planned actions and self-organising processes. The game could be used to explore how large chains such as Tesco grow to dominate grocery retailing. It would beneficial to test the game with a larger number of players – having only two retailers in South Yorkshire, as in the example we gave, is clearly unrealistic. Using the retail agent-based model as the basis for both systems subjected it to a lot of scrutiny and points to possible future improvements, such as retailer agents that take into account household accessibility levels, household density and/or household shopping budgets when deciding where to relocate. There is also a need to realistically calculate the attractiveness of clusters of shops all owned by the same chain-store retailer player. Disaggregating the household agents by different socio-economic variables might help to provide more realism.

In the ABM, the retailers followed dense residential areas and it was difficult to imagine any other distribution of retail given the static residential locations. These two subsystems are obviously closely linked, and it might be useful to build a more comprehensive version of the model in which households could also relocate. The game presented here provides players with complete and detailed information about the region, something that real retailers are unlikely to have access to. It might be interesting to experiment with giving players and agents partial information about the region to see how this affects the behaviour of individual players, and the region as a whole. Finally, there is potential to extend the game to work over a computer network to support larger numbers (ideally tens or hundreds) of players. This would provide more realistic conditions and responses for the simulation, as well as the opportunity to record and analyse human-agent-generated emergent patterns in the system. Berland and Rand (2009) see participatory simulations within an agent-based model framework as a way of 'crowdsourcing' dynamic information from participants. Players could take on a variety of different roles, including retailer, developer and planner. Supporting large numbers of players in this way is now almost routinely done in online games produced by the entertainment games industry.

References

Allen, P. M. and Sanglier, M. (1981) 'Urban evolution, self-organization, and decision making', *Environment and Planning A*, 13: 167–83.

Arthur, W. B. (1988) 'Urban systems and historical path dependence', in J. H. Ausubel and R. Herman (eds), *Cities and Their Vital Systems: Infrastructure, Past, Present and Future*, Washington, DC: National Academy Press, pp. 85–97.

Barreteau, O., Bousquet, F. and Attonaty, J. M. (2001) 'Role-playing games for opening the black box of multi-agent systems: Method and lessons of its application to Senegal River Valley irrigated systems', *Journal of Artificial Societies and Social Simulation*, 4: 5.

Batty, M., Steadman, P. and Xie, Y. (2004) *Visualization in Spatial Modeling*, CASA Working Paper 79, London: Centre for Advanced Spatial Analysis (UCL).

Berland, M. and Rand, W. (2009) 'Participatory simulation as a tool for agent-based simulation', Paper presented at *ICAART-09*, Porto, Portugal.

Cacciaguerra, S. and Roffilli, M. (2005) 'Agent-based participatory simulation activities for the emergence of complex social behaviours', Paper presented at *AISB Symposium on Socially Inspired Computing*, University of Hertfordshire.

Castella, J. C., Trung, T. N. and Boissau, S. (2005) 'Participatory simulation of land-use changes in the northern mountains of Vietnam: the combined use of an agent-based model, a role-playing game, and a geographic information system', *Ecology and Society*, 10: 27.

Garvin, A. (2001) *The American City: What Works, What Doesn't*, New York: John Wiley & Sons.

Hartmann, S. (1996) 'The world as a process: simulations in the natural and social sciences', in R. Hegselmann, U. Mueller and K. G. Troitzsch (eds), *Modelling and Simulation in the Social Sciences from a Philosophy of Science Point of View*, Dordrecht: Kluwer, pp. 77–100.

Jacobs, J. (1961) *The Death and Life of Great American Cities*, New York: Random House.

Kolb, D. A. (1984) *Experiential Learning: Experience as the Source of Learning and Development*, Englewood Cliffs, NJ, Prentice Hall.

Lobo, D. G. (2005) 'A city is not a toy: how SimCity plays with urbanism', Paper presented at *Discussion Paper Series, Cities Program, Architecture and Engineering*, London School of Economics and Political Science.

Macmillan, W. (1996) 'Fun and games: serious toys for city modelling in a GIS environment', in P. Longley and M. Batty (eds), *Spatial Analysis: Modelling in a GIS Environment*, Harlow: Longman, pp. 153–65.

Martine, G. (2007) *The State of the World Population 2007*, New York: United Nations Population Fund.

Mitchell, M. (2009) *Complexity: A Guided Tour*, New York: Oxford University Press.

Reckien, D. and Eisenack, K. (2008) 'Urban sprawl: using a game to sensitize stakeholders to the interdependencies among actors' preferences', *Simulation & Gaming*, 41: 260–77.

Schelling, T. C. (1969) 'Models of segregation', *The American Economic Review*, 59: 488–93.

Semboloni, F. (2007) 'The management of urban complexity through a multi-agent participatory simulation', *disP*, 170:57–70.

Squazzoni, F. (2008) 'The micro-macro link in social simulation', *Sociologica*, 2, available at: www.sociologica.mulino.it/journal/article/index/Article/Journal: ARTICLE:179 (accessed 30 September 2010).

Sterman, J. (1989) 'Modeling managerial behavior: misperceptions of feedback in a dynamic decision making experiment', *Management Science*, 35: 321–39.

Susi, T., Johannesson, M. and Backlund, P. (2007) *Serious Games – An Overview*, Skövde: School of Humanities and Informatics, University of Skövde, Sweden.

van Bilsen, A., Bekebrede, G. and Mayer, I. (2010) 'Understanding complex adaptive systems by playing games', *Informatics in Education*, 9: 1–18.

von Mammen, S. and Jacob, C. (2009) 'Swarming for games: immersion in complex systems', in M. Giacobini, A. Fink and F. Rothlauf *et al.* (eds), *Applications of Evolutionary Computing*, Berlin: Springer, pp. 293–302.

Vonk, G., Geertman, S. and Schot, P. (2005) 'Bottlenecks blocking widespread usage of planning support systems', *Environment and Planning A*, 37: 909–24.

Weaver, W. (1948) 'Science and complexity', *American Scientist*, 36: 536–44.
Wilensky, U. and Stroup, W. (1999) 'Learning through participatory simulations: network-based design for systems learning in classrooms', Paper presented at *Computer Supported Collaborative Learning Conference*, Stanford University.
Wilson, A. G. (2008) 'Boltzmann, Lotka and Volterra and spatial structural evolution: an integrated methodology for some dynamical systems', *Journal of the Royal Society, Interface*, 5: 865–71.

7   Applications in archaeology and history

7.1 Introduction

Geography is rooted in place and archaeology and history in time.[1] But the interesting questions in geography are about change, and history, especially a sub-discipline such as urban history, is sometimes focused on place. A more common distinction is that geographers, on the whole, work in contemporary times and historians in past times, though this distinction is blurred by the work of historical geographers, on the one hand, and contemporary historians, on the other. Perhaps – a conjecture – one reason why the two disciplines do not come closer together is because the data available from historical sources are so imperfect that the techniques of the contemporary geographer seem unusable. History is a jigsaw puzzle with many of the pieces missing.

The geographical modeller can offer, first, a systematic framework for analysis that embraces both place and time, and, second, models based on this framework that may be used, in some instances, to fill in data gaps. The framework itself offers a way of systematising the historical 'picture' and integrating historical evidence, and the models, through the theories on which they are built, can offer new insights for historians. Thus, it is possible to articulate a common foundation and to facilitate ongoing research. The aim in this paper is to show, through two case studies, how ideas developed in geographical modelling can be generalised for the potential benefit of both archaeology and history.

The models to be developed have an important role to play in complexity science. Weaver (1948, 1958) characterised problems – or systems – as simple, of disorganised complexity and of organised complexity, and the models presented here lie in the third category, with sub-models developed from the second. In particular, they exhibit non-linearities and the characteristics of such systems come into play – particularly the notion of 'path dependence'.

7.2 Geographical models

7.2.1 Introduction

It is useful to begin by briefly referring to the classical models that geographers have typically brought to bear and that are still much cited, and then to outline a newer (though now not-so-new) generation of mathematical models. It can be shown that the classical models are special cases of these.

The models can relate to towns, cities, regions or even countries, and the flows between them. Or we can examine interactions between zones in a smaller area, such as a single town.

7.2.2 The classical models

The candidate models are:

- Malthus – demography;
- Von Thünen – agricultural land use;
- Weber – location of industry;
- Palander, Hoover and Hotelling – market areas and competing firms;
- Burgess, Hoyt, Harris and Ullman – urban structure and development – residential structures;
- Christaller and Losch – central place theory; and
- Zipf – spatial interaction.

Interestingly, these models are all defined on a basis that treats space as continuous. They define their own boundaries. The mathematical models to be presented here work best when space is divided into a set of discrete zones. This may indicate that the deployment of this kind of zone system was a powerful invention!

Malthus (1798) demographic model offered exponential growth and then corresponding decline as resources became unavailable. This model became the logistic model. Von Thünen's (1826) work on agricultural land use remains very important, partly because it was fully rooted in its historical period – more importantly because it opened up some valuable economic concepts in urban and regional analysis. He showed that by introducing transport costs, the more intensive agriculture would be found in rings near to markets. These ideas were generalised in a contemporary context by Alonso (1964) and cast in mathematical programming form by Herbert and Stevens (1960). Weber's (1909) work on industrial location was similarly important. He was concerned with the optimum location of a factory in relation to resources, labour and markets. These concepts were generalised in different ways by Palander (1935), Hoover (1937) and Hotelling (1929). Burgess (1927), Hoyt (1939) and Harris and Ullman (1945) were all concerned with the social structure of cities. Burgess showed how immigrants took up residence in inner-city areas and progressively, as wealth increased, moved further out: another kind of ring structure. Hoyt added a sector dimension, and Harris and Ullman a poly-nucleated structure. Christaller (1933) and Losch (1940), in different ways, set themselves the task of modelling the overall pattern of villages, towns and cities in relation to market areas, based on different principles. Zipf (1946) developed a model of spatial interaction by analogy with Newton's law of gravity.

All of these models offer some insights and the beginnings of theories in their various domains. However, it can be shown that, within the mathematical modelling formalism introduced here, all of these models can be reproduced as special cases – see Wilson (2000) for a review of these developments. In this chapter, we focus on one particular model from the set that is available and show how it can be transported from contemporary analysis into, first, archaeology and, then, history. The two case studies to be presented are based on the model that has been extensively used in earlier chapters.

7.3 Archaeology

In the late 1980s, Rihll and Wilson (1987a, 1987b, 1991) worked with point data on urban structures in Greece in the ninth century BC. Locations were known from archaeological explorations, but nothing was known of relative sizes. This work is now being developed further.[2] See Figure 7.1 for a map of the settlement locations.

Figure 7.1 Settlements in Greece in the ninth century BC

The retail model was reinterpreted. The i's and j's in the model can now be taken as settlement locations and the interactions a combination of trade and migration. It is then possible to run the model with, initially, 'all settlement sizes equal' – that is, all the W_js equal – and to seek an equilibrium from the dynamic equations – essentially solving Equation 7.9 below iteratively. In this case, with very sparse data, it was necessary to explore a range of α and β parameter values to see if plausible outcomes could be achieved. One set of results is shown in Figure 7.2.

Bevan has now improved the network base of the model to take topography into account, as shown in Figure 7.3. This is an elementary network analysis to show the hierarchical structure that emerged – and it is interesting that the main central places include Athens, Corinth and Thebes. These central places were all well known to archaeologists bar one, and it is probably still an open question as to whether a major dig should be launched there!

What this illustrates is that models can help to solve 'missing data' problems – and this is likely to be very helpful in archaeological and historical contexts.

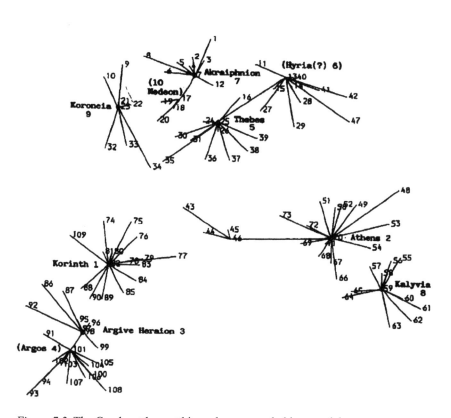

Figure 7.2 The Greek settlement hierarchy as revealed in a model run

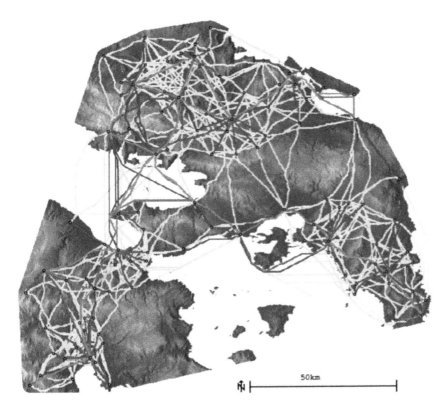

Figure 7.3 A more realistic network with modelled flows[3]

7.4 History

7.4.1 Introduction

The second example takes us beyond equilibrium analysis to attempt to model real dynamics: the evolution of the United States regional system from 1790 to 1870. The period was chosen because, first, there was good census data on urban populations and, second, we were particularly interested in the impact of railway development on the Midwest, following the work of Cronon (1991). The exploration of the evolution of systems of cities has a long history – illustrated by Berry's (1964) classic paper. In this section, we take a simple model based on that used for the evolution of retail centres *within* a city and reinterpret it as a model of a *system* of cities. The retail model is outlined again for convenience in Section 7.4.2, and its 'system' interpretation in Section 7.4.3. In Section 7.4.4, we explain the idea of urban 'DNA' and its evolution. In Section 7.4.5, we describe the current system of interest – the evolution of Chicago from 1790 to 1870 in the context of the development of the United States in that period, with particular reference to railways. We present some results to explore the evolution of the populations of cities in this system in Section 7.4.6. There are many possible avenues for further research, and these are discussed in Section 7.4.7.

7.4.2 The retail model

The simple aggregated retail model of previous chapters is repeated here for convenience. $S_{ij}(t)$ is the flow of spending from residents of i to shops in j at time t. In this case, we add a t label to the remaining definitions to prepare the way for building a dynamic model. Let $e_i(t)$ be spending per head and $P_i(t)$ the population of i. The parameter $c_{ij}(t)$ is the travel cost from zone i to zone j at time t. $W_j(t)$ is a measure of the attractiveness of shops in j, which, for these illustrative purposes, we take as the logarithm of 'size' – reflecting range of choice and lower prices through scale economies. The obvious order parameter would be $N(W_j > 0)$ – the number of centres that are non-zero. In a fully dispersed system, then $N(W_j > 0)$ would be equal to the number of possible centres and would be large, while in a very centralised system $N(W_j > 0)$ would be 1.

The usual model with a time label added is then:

$$S_{ij}(t) = A_i(t)\, e_i(t)\, P_i(t)\, W_j(t)^{\alpha(t)} \, \exp\left(-\beta(t)\, c_{ij}(t)\right) \tag{7.1}$$

where:

$$A_i(t) = \frac{1}{\sum_k W_k(t)^{\alpha(t)} \, \exp\left(-\beta(t)\, c_{ik}(t)\right)} \tag{7.2}$$

to ensure that:

$$\sum_j S_{ij}(t) = e_i(t)\, P_i(t) \tag{7.3}$$

and:

$$\sum_{ij} S_{ij}(t)\, \log W_j(t) = X(t) \tag{7.4}$$

where $\log W_j(t)$, as we noted earlier, is taken as the measure of consumer benefits and $X(t)$ an estimate of the total benefits achieved. We also have:

$$\sum_{ij} S_{ij}(t)\, c_{ij}(t) = C(t) \tag{7.5}$$

$\alpha(t)$ and $\beta(t)$ are parameters (actually, the Lagrangian multipliers associated with Equations 7.4 and 7.5). Because the matrix is only constrained at the origin end, we can calculate the total flows into destinations as:

$$D_j(t) = \sum_i S_{ij}(t) = \sum_i \left[\frac{e_i(t)\, P_i(t)\, W_j(t)^{\alpha(t)} \, \exp\left(-\beta(t)\, c_{ij}(t)\right)}{\sum_k W_k(t)^{\alpha(t)} \, \exp\left(-\beta(t)\, c_{ik}(t)\right)} \right] \tag{7.6}$$

A suitable hypothesis for representing the dynamics is:

$$\Delta W_j(t, t+1) = \varepsilon(t) \left[D_j(t) - K(t) W_j(t) \right] \tag{7.7}$$

where $K(t)$ is such that $K(t)W_j(t)$ can be taken as the (notional) cost of running the shopping centre in j. This equation then says that if the centre is profitable, it grows; if not, it declines. The parameter ε determines the speed of response to these signals.

The equilibrium position is given by:

$$D_j(t) = K(t) W_j(t) \tag{7.8}$$

which can be written out in full as:

$$\sum_i \left[\frac{e_i(t) P_i(t) W_j(t)^{\alpha(t)} \exp\left(-\beta(t) c_{ij}(t)\right)}{\sum_k W_k(t)^{\alpha(t)} \exp\left(-\beta(t) c_{ik}(t)\right)} \right] = K(t) W_j(t) \tag{7.9}$$

and these are clearly non-linear simultaneous equations in the $\{W_j(t)\}$.

The dynamics are given by:

$$W_j(t+1) = W_j(t) + \Delta W_j(t, t+1) \tag{7.10}$$

If the populations and the total floor space do not change, then Equations 7.7 and 7.10 simply represent moves towards equilibrium.

7.4.3 Reinterpreting and extending the model for a system of cities

We now assume that each node in the system is a city (or a town or a village) with population P_i and level of economic activity W_i. e_i is the average level of economic activity generated per capita and S_{ij} represents the level of interaction between places – to be interpreted mainly as trade flows – but with an accompanying implicit assumption, which we will formulate formally below, that migration follows trade. c_{ij} is a measure of transport cost as usual and K_i is a measure of the cost per unit of maintaining a level of economic activity at i. We will have the possibility of e_i representing a spectrum from poor to rich, and similarly, K_i, from cheap to expensive, and so in a sense reflecting 'rent'.

A particularly interesting development is to examine the dynamics of $\{c_{ij}\}$, and here we do this exogenously using an underlying spider network. It is interesting and important to do this as an extension of the usual model, but also because it may be critical to the evolution of the system around Chicago.

For the total population, for illustration, we can assume an annual rate of increase – say from net migration and births over deaths, of, say, λ_p, from t to $t+1$ for each t. We can obviously vary this assumption. We also ought to introduce some 'noise' into the system. However, the key assumption we make is that the change in population at i is determined by the change in the level of economic activity. We can combine these assumptions as follows:

$$P_i(t+1) = \mu(t)\left[P_i(t)(1+\phi_{1i}) + \phi_2 \Delta W_i(t,\, t+1)\right] \tag{7.11}$$

where ϕ_{1t} is a random variable, suitably scaled, with a mean considerably less than 1, ϕ_2 is a constant that represents the scale of population change related to change in economic activity (which can be positive or negative) and $\mu(t)$ is a normalising factor to ensure that the overall growth rate is λ_t. Hence:

$$\sum_i P_i(t+1) = \left(1+\lambda_t\right)\sum_i P_i(t) \tag{7.12}$$

so that $\mu(t)$ is determined from:

$$\mu(t)\sum_i\left[P_i(t)(1+\phi_{1i}) + \phi_2 \Delta W_i(t,\, t+1)\right] = \sum_i\left(1+\lambda_t\right)P_i(t) \tag{7.13}$$

and hence:

$$\mu(t) = \frac{\sum_i\left(1+\lambda_t\right)P_i(t)}{\sum_i\left[P_i(t)(1+\phi_{1i}) + \phi_2 \Delta W_i(t,\, t+1)\right]} \tag{7.14}$$

The model would then be run by working through Equations 7.1, 7.2, 7.6, 7.7, 7.9[4] and 7.10, and then adjusting $\{P_i\}$ through Equation 7.11, and recycling through Equations 7.1, 7.2, 7.6, 7.7, 7.9 and 7.10 with $P_i(t+1)$.

7.4.4 System 'DNA' and its evolution

It is well known that the pattern of evolution of a dynamical system – the core of the dynamical model in our case being Equations 7.7, 7.10 and 7.11 – are strongly dependent on the initial conditions. In the case of urban and regional systems, it has been argued (Wilson 2008) that for each step in the evolution of a dynamical system represented by these kinds of difference equations, the 'initial conditions' at time t, as determinants of the equations solutions at time $t+1$, can be regarded as the 'DNA' of the system. This is because since the changes in a step are likely to be relatively small, the possibilities of change – what might be called the 'cone of possible development' – will be strongly determined by what is there. This accords with a common-sense view of the situation: that the existing infrastructure, economic activities and populations will determine what is possible in the immediate future. In the model presented here, therefore, the 'DNA' can be taken as a string – the set of scalars, vectors and matrices:

$$\left[\{e_i\},\, \{P_i\},\, \{W_j\},\, \{c_{ij}\},\, \{K_i\},\, \{\alpha\},\, \{\beta\},\, \{\lambda_i\},\, \{\phi_1\},\, \{\phi_2\}\right] \tag{7.15}$$

The *i*-elements:

$$\left[e_i, P_i, W_i, c_{ij} \text{(for all } j\text{)}, K_i, \alpha, \beta, \lambda_t, \phi_1, \phi_2 \right] \tag{7.16}$$

can be taken as the 'DNA' characteristics of the zone and can be used to build typologies.

As the system evolves over time, the DNA also evolves. This represents the slow dynamics of the system. It is the $\{S_{ij}\}$ that represents the fast dynamics of the system – the 'physiology'. It is already clear that in the model, some of the DNA variables are exogenous and some are endogenous. The model will predict the evolution of the endogenous elements with the timelines of the other elements specified outside the model. The ambition in model development is always to extend the list of endogenous variables and to minimise the extent of the exogenous ones.

The model can, in principle, be used in three ways: first, to seek to explain the evolution of a system of interest – and this is where it is potentially of interest to historical geography. Second, to establish typologies based on the DNA. Third, in a contemporary planning context to explore 'genetic medicine': how can the DNA string be modified to take the system to a desired path outside the cone of possible development? In the rest of the chapter, we focus on the first of these objectives, and take as our system of interest the evolution of the regional system around Chicago from 1790 through the nineteenth century.

7.4.5 The system of interest

Chicago and its wider environs make an excellent case study, and there is a very good history (Cronon 1991) on which we have relied heavily. Population census data is available for each decade from 1790, and in our model each iteration represents one year. There is rapid development much influenced by changes in transport technology, notably the building of railway lines. Since we are interested in both the opening up of the Midwest and the access to markets in the Northeast, we consider a large region for our system of interest, as shown in Figure 7.4.

The data (or the assumptions when data is not available) for the model runs is assembled as follows. Population data (P_i) is obtained from the NHGIS census website at www.nhgis.org. We used county data collected every decade of our study period, and since the county boundaries changed on a regular basis, we aggregated the data to a 120 km square grid to achieve period-by-period consistency (Figure 7.5). The centroid of each grid square (after being cropped by water boundaries) is then taken as the position of an aggregate settlement, which is representative of the whole grid square area. The initial values for each P_i come from the 1790 census.

The economic activity per capita, e_i, was set to \$500. We assumed one-third of the population would be employed in any given settlement and so the initial value for each W_j was set to one-third of P_i (taking W_j as a count of the number of jobs in a zone). In order to maintain a constant ratio of 3:1 in population versus jobs, we recalculate the number of jobs in a settlement after calculating the normalised population dynamics:

$$W_i(t) = \frac{P_i(t)}{3} \qquad (7.17)$$

K_i was set to a constant value K calculated from:

$$K = \frac{\sum_i e_i P_i}{\sum_i W_i} \qquad (7.18)$$

The transport costs (c_{ij}) are calculated on the basis of lowest 'cost' routes through a spider network using Dijkstra's (1959) algorithm. There are three kinds of links: roads, water and rail, with rail links further subdivided into branch and trunk lines. We upgrade specific links at the appropriate iteration in a model run to represent railway construction. The links are weighted through three parameters: if road distance in km is the unit, then a water link is multiplied by w, say, a branch rail link by r and trunk lines by t. In the tests presented below, w is taken as 1/16 and

Figure 7.4 Model area with Midwest boundary

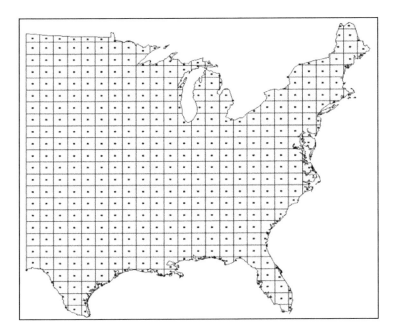

Figure 7.5 The grid of aggregated settlements

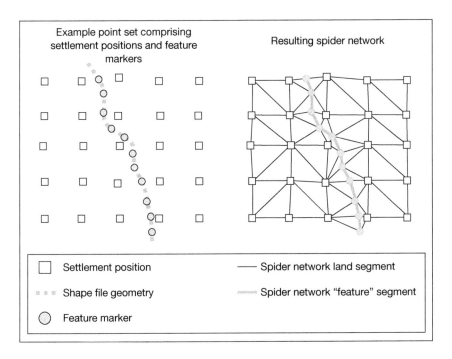

Figure 7.6 A method for adding shape file features into the spider network

r as 1/20 and *t* as 1/40. We construct the spider network by calculating a Delaunay (1934) triangulation of the aggregated settlement positions together with additional points that mark the path of water and railways. These additional points are derived from shape files of appropriate data (i.e. rivers, lakes, coastline and railways) and the general method, applicable to all kinds of data, is illustrated in Figure 7.6. Full details of the spider network construction are given in Appendix 7.1. The spider network around Chicago is shown in Figure 7.7, and the full spider network is shown in Figure 7.8.

The model parameters α, β, ε, ϕ_1, ϕ_2, w, r and t were estimated by a combination of manual and automated calibration, which aimed to maximise the average *R*-squared value for the whole 80-year period when comparing the model output to the census data for the appropriate year – in order to obtain year-by-year census records, we interpolated between the nearest two decades. The national increase in population for each iteration, λ_i, was also calculated from the interpolated year-by-year census records.

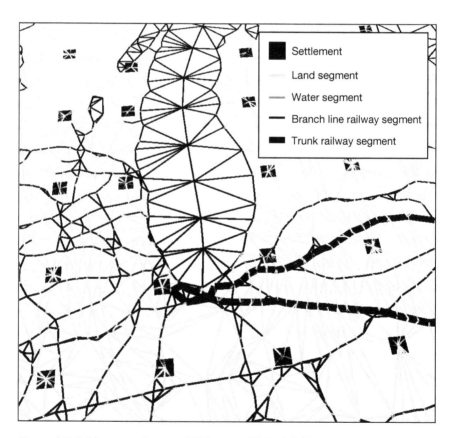

Figure 7.7 Spider network around Chicago and Lake Michigan

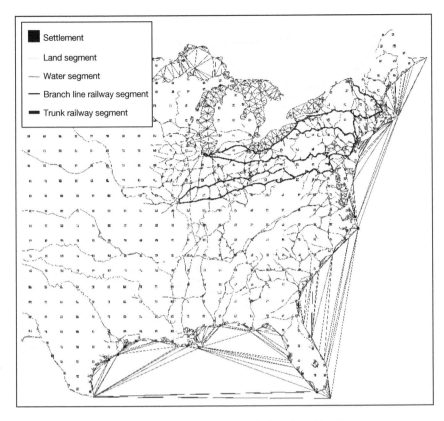

Figure 7.8 The complete spider network for 1870 showing all rail lines

7.4.6 Results

The best-fit model parameters below gave an average R-squared over all 80 years of ~0.24:

- $\alpha = 0.26$
- $\beta = 0.03$
- $\varepsilon = 0.0006$
- $\phi_1 = 0.01$
- $\phi_2 = 3$
- $w = 0.06$
- $r = 0.05$
- $t = 0.025$

The Chicago grid square population was 264,546 compared to 456,959 in the census data giving an error of –192,413. Figure 7.9 shows four evenly spaced years from the best-fit model run. From 1791 until 1840, growth in the model is mainly confined to the east coast, with some small settlements also appearing along the south coast. Here, the model output is less concentrated in the north than the census data, and this may be because we do not model the influence of seaports such as New York – a possible future model improvement. In the early 1840s, we see growth following the construction of the railway lines westwards, and this intensifies so that by 1870, a new transport corridor exists between New York and the Midwest, along which large settlements have developed, representing a major change to the distribution of economic activity in the country. Appendix 7.2 provides a comparison of the model population and census data for each decade between 1790 and 1870. The model also offers estimates of the trade flows between zones, and in Figure 7.10 we show the flows from Chicago for 1971 and 1870.

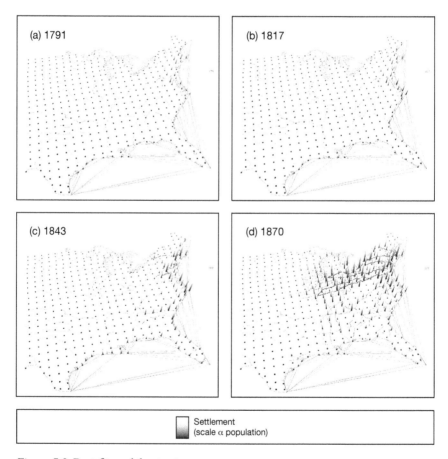

Figure 7.9 Best-fit model output

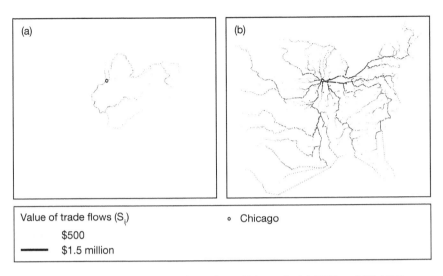

Figure 7.10 Predictions of export flows from Chicago in (a) 1791 and (b) 1870

7.4.7 Concluding comments

There are many possible improvements that can be explored with this type of model in future work, and we conclude by outlining some of these. We explore disaggregation and we indicate how the attractiveness factor could be expanded. We explore the challenge of modelling transport system dynamics.

In the model as presented, W_j is taken as an aggregate measure of economic activity. In practice, there are at least four markets that make up this aggregate, and we need to explore at some point treating these separately. They are: grain, livestock and meat packing, lumber, and manufactured goods. The first three are exports from the Midwest, particularly to the Northeast. The last is made up of exports from the Northeast, some of which are imports to the Midwest. This last is complicated by the fact that much of the distribution to small towns and settlements was by the newly invented mail order. If the volumes in each case could be translated into value, then there would be common units to produce an aggregate value. Alternatively, the model could be run for the four markets separately or re-aggregated, as indicated in the next subsection, through the attractiveness function.

There are at least two ways of disaggregating the attractiveness function (and, indeed, these two ways could be used in combination). In each case, W_j would be broken down into a series of multiplicative factors:

$$W_j^\alpha = W_j^{(1)^{\alpha(1)}} W_j^{(2)^{\alpha(2)}} W_j^{(3)^{\alpha(3)}} \qquad (7.19)$$

Each $W_j^{(k)}$ with ($k = 1, 2, 3, 4$) could be taken as attractiveness factors for each of the four markets: grain, livestock/meat, lumber and manufactured goods, or it could be taken to represent different influences, such as level of economic development or technological advances – such as grain silos and 'booster' marketing of some of the cities.

The railway lines have been entered exogenously for our model runs. More ambitiously, we could attempt to model the evolution of the transport network by adding a dynamic hypothesis, which would be the transport system equivalent of Equation 7.7. A conjecture for this might be:

$$\Delta c_{ij} = \mu \left[S_{ij}(t+1) - S_{ij}(t) \right] \tag{7.20}$$

However, the task is more complicated than this. A real transport network is made up of links, and a new railway line, for example, is a sequence of links in the network. Each link carries traffic from many origin-destination pairs, and so there is an issue of whether we should try to reformulate Equation 7.20 on a link basis rather than an origin-destination basis.

The results that have been presented are offered on a 'proof of concept' basis: this is a potentially interesting way to explore historical geography. It is well known that the evolution of non-linear dynamical systems is path dependent. We have introduced the idea of 'system DNA' as the sequence of initial conditions for the slow dynamics of our system of interest and we have paid particular attention to the changes in travel costs brought about by the introduction of railways. This shows how the acts of individuals – in this case, the railway developers – influence the evolutionary path of the system of interest. Given that the model is a very simple and crude one, the fact that the results fit the data tolerably well suggests that this might be a rich seam for further exploration.

7.5 Concluding comments

The models introduced here are at the core of geographical theory, but make use of ideas from economics, physics, ecology and political science, and are shown to have applications in archaeology and history. This epitomises what can be achieved through interdisciplinary thinking. The umbrella for these kinds of concepts in contemporary research is provided by complexity science. In the future, there is no doubt that this toolkit will expand and there will be a much wider range of application.

Appendix 7.1 Spider network construction

The spider network was constructed by calculating a Delaunay triangulation of a set of points comprising the settlement positions and some additional feature markers. The feature markers were derived from shape files of appropriate data, including rivers, lakes, coastline and railways. Each feature marker was given a type indicating the kind of feature it represented, either water or rail. Railway feature markers additionally contained data on year of construction. The network links produced by the Delaunay triangulation were given their type based on the rules that took into account the type of the two end points and the position of the link in relation to the original shape file features.

Appendix 7.2 Comparison of model output with census data

This section contains a decade-by-decade comparison of the best-fit model output with the census data.

Figure 7.11 Aggregated 1790 census data

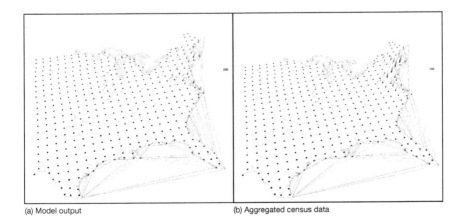

(a) Model output   (b) Aggregated census data

Figure 7.12 Comparison of model with census data for 1800

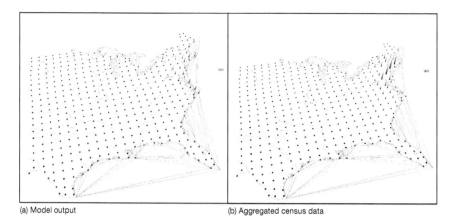

(a) Model output   (b) Aggregated census data

Figure 7.13 Comparison of model with census data for 1810

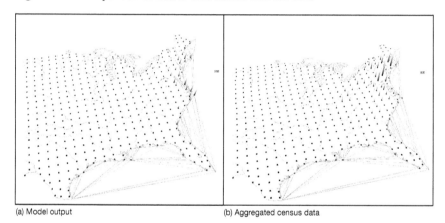

(a) Model output   (b) Aggregated census data

Figure 7.14 Comparison of model with census data for 1820

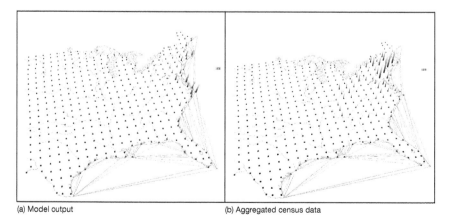

(a) Model output   (b) Aggregated census data

Figure 7.15 Comparison of model with census data for 1830

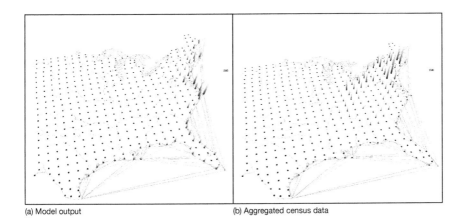

(a) Model output   (b) Aggregated census data

Figure 7.16 Comparison of model with census data for 1840

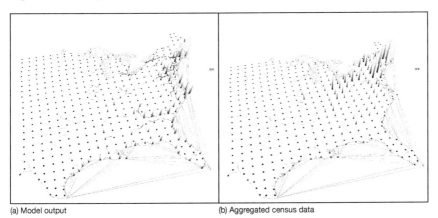

(a) Model output   (b) Aggregated census data

Figure 7.17 Comparison of model with census data for 1850

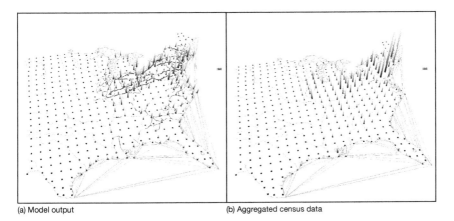

(a) Model output   (b) Aggregated census data

Figure 7.18 Comparison of model with census data for 1860

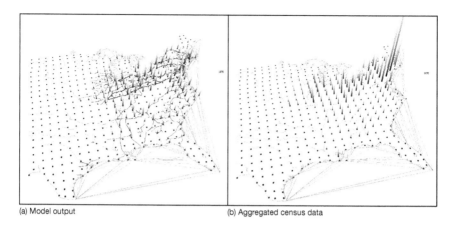

(a) Model output   (b) Aggregated census data

Figure 7.19 Comparison of model with census data for 1870

Notes

1   Henceforth, for convenience, I will simply use 'history' for 'archaeology and history'.
2   A. Bevan, private communication.
3   I am grateful to Andrew Bevan for this figure.
4   Implying that we run the W_j system to equilibrium using an inner loop every iteration of the model.

References

Alonso, W. (1964) *Location and Land Use*, Cambridge, MA: Harvard University Press.
Berry, B. J. L. (1964) 'Cities as systems within systems of cities', *Papers of the Regional Science Association*, 13(1): 146–63.
Burgess, E. W. (1927) 'The determinants of gradients in the growth of a city', *Publications, American Sociological Society*, 21: 178–84.
Christaller, W. (1933) *Die centralen Orte in Suddeutschland*, Jena: Gustav Fischer; translated by Baskin, C. W., *Central Places in Southern Germany*, Englewood Cliffs, NJ: Prentice Hall.
Cronon, W. (1991) *Nature's Metropolis: Chicago and the Great West*, New York: W. W. Norton.
Delaunay, B. (1934), 'Sur La Sphere Vide', *Izv. Akad. Nauk SSSR Otdel. Mat. Est. Nauk*, 7: 793–800.
Dijkstra, E. W. (1959), 'A note on two problems in connexion with graphs', *Numerische Mathematik*, 1: 269–71.
Harris, C. D. and Ullman, E. L. (1945) 'The nature of cities', *Annals, American Academy of Political and Social Sciences*, 242: 7–17.
Herbert, D. J. and Stevens, B. H. (1960) 'A model for the distribution of residential activity in an urban area', *Journal of Regional Science*, 2: 21–36.
Hoover, E. M. (1937) *Location Theory and the Shoe and Leather Industries*, Cambridge, MA: Harvard University Press.

Hotelling, H. (1929) 'Stability in competition', *Economic Journal*, 39: 41–57.

Hoyt, H. (1939) *The Structure and Growth of Residential Neighbourhoods in American Cities*, Washington, DC: Federal Housing Administration.

Losch, A. (1940) *Die raumliche ordnung der wirtschaft*, Jena: Gustav Fischer; translated by Woglam, W. H. and Stolper, W. F. (1954) *The Economics of Location*, New Haven, CT: Yale University Press.

Malthus, T. R. (1798) *An Essay on the Principle of Population*, London: J. Johnson.

Palander, T. (1935) *Beitrage zur standortstheorie*, Uppsala: Almquist & Wiksell.

Rihll, T. E. and Wilson, A. G. (1987a) 'Spatial interaction and structural models in historical analysis: some possibilities and an example', *Histoire et Mesure*, II(1): 5–32.

Rihll, T. E. and Wilson, A. G. (1987b) 'Model-based approaches to the analysis of regional settlement structures: the case of ancient Greece', in P. Denley and D. Hopkin (eds), *History and Computing*, Manchester: Manchester University Press, pp. 10–20.

Rihll, T. E. and Wilson, A. G. (1991) 'Settlement structures in ancient Greece: new approaches to the polis', in J. Rich and A. Wallace-Hadrill (eds), *City and Country in the Ancient World*, London: Croom Helm, pp. 58–95.

Von Thünen, J. H. (1826) *Der isolierte staat in beziehung auf landwirtschaft und nationalokonomie*, Stuttgart: Gustav Fisher; English translation by C. M. Wartenburg (1966) *The Isolated State*, Oxford: Oxford University Press.

Weaver, W. (1948) 'Science and complexity', *American Scientist*, 36: 536–44.

Weaver, W. (1958) 'A quarter century in the natural sciences', *Annual Report, The Rockefeller Foundation*, New York, pp. 7–122.

Weber, A. (1909) *Uber den standort der industrien*, Tübingen; English translation by C. J. Friedrich, *Theory of the Location of Industries*, Chicago, IL: University of Chicago Press.

Wilson, A. G. (2000) *Complex spatial systems*, Harlow: Addison-Wesley-Longman.

Wilson, A. G. (2008) 'Boltzmann, Lotka and Volterra and spatial structural evolution: an integrated methodology for some dynamical systems', *Journal of the Royal Society, Interface*, 5: 865–71.

Zipf, G. K. (1946) 'The P1P2/D hypothesis on the inter-city movement of persons', *American Sociological Review*, 11: 677–86.

8   Research challenges

8.1 Towards realistic models

All the models described in this book are offered on a 'proof-of-concept' basis. The construction and analysis of dynamic models shows that considerable progress has been made: phase changes can be identified; the nature of path dependence unpicked; and the possible uses of such models in planning illustrated through the idea of 'DNA' and 'possibility cones'. An obvious next step is to make the models more realistic, typically through disaggregation. This has been done extensively in the spatial interaction component of the retail model (Birkin *et al.* 1996). In the aggregate model used in earlier chapters, for example, the aggregate flow matrix $\{S_{ij}\}$ could be replaced by $\{S_{ij}^{kwn}\}$, say, where k was a person type, w, income and n, retail centre type (or more likely, in real applications, a store type). Such disaggregation complicates the dynamics, of course, but can also lead to new kinds of interesting results. In the retail case, with the model functioning at the store level, it may be possible to identify vulnerable companies, for example. In the model based on Lowry principles in Chapter 4, we did develop a disaggregate model, and this allowed us to show how house types that had been associated with lower incomes could be 'taken over' by those with higher – the 'gentrification' process. This model also begins to show the effects of subsystem linkages on dynamics and also offers new indicators such as 'housing pressure', which could then be related to the land market and associated housing prices. In the case of the Chicago model in Chapter 7, it would obviously be fruitful to disaggregate in terms of the main components of trade – grain, livestock and meat packing, lumber and manufactured goods. There is substantial scope for further research on these lines.

In the early stages of model development, it is sometimes necessary to treat some features and associated variables as exogenous either through lack of data or, more often perhaps, because of model development challenges. A good example is provided by the Chicago model in Chapter 7, where the evolution of the rail network is input exogenously. A research challenge is to make this endogenous. This has been achieved in a contemporary road transport model, and could, in principle, be extended to more complex situations (de Martinis *et al.* 2014).

8.2 Technical challenges

While we believe that we have successfully opened up some significant avenues of research, we are conscious that increased computing power and new data sources will create new opportunities. For example, even our South Yorkshire retail model functions in a 19-dimensional phase space, and large numbers of computer runs are needed to explore, for example, how basins of attraction 'move' as parameters change. This kind of knowledge is potentially valuable for planners and developers, and so there is an associated visualisation and presentation challenge.

There is a further 'high dimensionality' issue: we have illustrated the complications of path dependence – a sequence of 'initial conditions. The array of initial conditions is formidable, and representing the 'cones of possibility', for example, is a serious visualisation challenge. We could, in principle, show how, in relation to initial conditions at any point in time, these relate to critical size markers of the kind introduced in Chapter 2.

We have presented a results grid as the basis for model calibration, and this works well when we have two principal parameters. As models are disaggregated, the number of parameters will increase and we will need new methods – 'big computing' – to optimise the calibration process.

This list, potentially, can all be handled in terms of increased computing power. We can then look further ahead: as relevant data become available in real time – for example, the possibility of estimating the $\{c_{ij}\}$ array from Google Maps – we can seek to calibrate models through real time, at each point analysing dynamic 'pressures' and underlying basins of attraction.

8.3 Applications in planning

Models have been used extensively in planning, but by no means comprehensively or even 'typically'. Most planners do not use models in their work, and there is considerable scope for further research here. The models are most developed for planning purposes in retail and transport planning, though there have been some good applications with Lowry-based models. However, these applications have always been concerned with the relatively short term and using models in a comparative static-equilibrium mode – essentially (and simplifying) the spatial interaction component without the dynamics.

The conceptualisation of the 'models in planning' process is illustrated in Figure 8.1 (Roumpani and Wilson 2014). This illustrates the different kinds of data potentially available – on the left side of the diagram. This has to be processed in various ways to construct an information system that is at the heart of the process. The modeller-planner can extract from the information system inputs to specify a model run, receive reports (in the illustration in this figure from ESRI's City Engine), the output of which feeds back into the information system for (if required) ongoing access and use. By working iteratively, the planner can 'design' with the aid of models by adjusting the controllable exogenous variables.

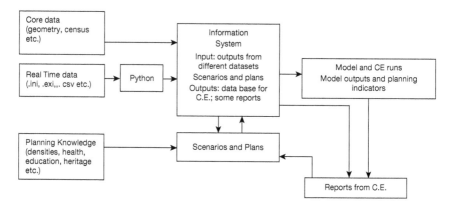

Figure 8.1 An interactive modelling and planning system using City Engine

There are essentially three modes of use:

1   evaluating a current situation by calculating indicators and identifying challenges – essentially exploring the current equilibrium – and this is enhanced by being in a dynamic framework because new indicators are available, such as housing pressure;
2   testing plans for the short run (e.g. for significant new housing developments); and
3   exploring long-run scenarios.

In modes 1 and 2, the principal contribution from dynamic modelling is through the development of new indicators that are significant even for the analysis of an equilibrium situation. For mode 3, for long-run explorations, a timeline of exogenous variables will be input by the planner, some of these such as population projections forming a core 'backcloth', some, such as allocations of housing, 'planning design' variables, that can be chosen. A dynamic model can then illustrate possible development paths – the 'cones of possibility' of Chapter 3 – and the ideas of 'urban DNA' and 'genetic planning' can be deployed. All of this represents new territory and a major research challenge.

8.4 Applications across scales and times

The analysis presented in this book has been based on a relatively small number of examples. However, it is clear that the core ideas are applicable to any system whose elements satisfy the conditions for which Boltzmann and Lotka-Volterra principles hold: a large weakly interacting 'population' generating flows between 'origins' and 'destinations', and where there are 'facilities' at the destination end that are competing for 'business' (or where the populations are competing for spaces in the facilities). Inverted commas have been deployed around the key generic terms here because each can be interpreted very widely. We have shown how models can be developed in a variety of circumstances through our examples, but it is clear intuitively that the range of possible application is much broader.

A number of examples can already be identified: international trade and the impact of changing technologies – larger ships and ports; migration flows; and, perhaps most interestingly, applications to war and battles – both contemporary and historical. In this last case, spatial interaction is interpreted as 'threat', which, particularly in historical examples, attenuates with distance. The well-known Richardson (1960) models of arms races can be given spatial dimensions along the lines of the examples already presented here.

More broadly, there are many disciplines that satisfy the Boltzmann-Lotka-Volterra conditions. Examples can be found in most of the social sciences, and, as we have seen, in archaeology and history, where it is clear that there is a very wide range of potential examples.

8.5 Greater challenges

The challenges identified above build directly on the research outlined in the book. For the longer run, greater challenges can be already identified:

1   In the search for more realistic models, the drive is always towards greater disaggregation, and this generates a very high level of dimensionality – arrays with many subscripts and superscripts. It was once estimated that, even with quite coarse categories, as many as 10^{13} variables might be needed for a comprehensive description of an urban system (Wilson 2007). One way to handle this is through micro-simulation – a method that generates a hypothetical population that 'looks like' a real one through the use of conditional probability distributions that are consistent with the data. The challenge in the context of this book is to further develop the present range of micro-simulation models and to make them fully dynamic.

2   This connects to deeper theory development to underpin the models. Articulating the structures in terms of conditional probabilities is, in effect, specifying 'chains of causality', and this process needs to be thought through systematically.

3   Most of our examples have been constructed using Boltzmann-style spatial interaction models with a Lotka-Volterra element added. As we have seen, the Boltzmann represents the fast dynamics, the Lotka-Volterra the slow. In the Lotka-Volterra case, what are being generated are structures that evolve over time. There are other approaches to modelling the evolution of structure – notably, that first introduced by Turing in the context of morphogenesis, involving two or more diffusion equations that interact to generate the structures.

4   We have already seen that there are alternative modelling 'styles', particularly agent-based modelling and gaming – and we have shown how these can be adapted to the problems of this book in Chapters 5 and 6. There are clearly many opportunities to develop these ideas further, not least to formally demonstrate equivalences. We can add to this list cellular automata modelling

and various kinds of economic models. Since, in all cases, we are seeking to model the same real systems, integration should be possible but has not yet been achieved.

8.6 Concluding comments: combinatorial evolution

A meta-research task that is likely to be productive is to seek to frame the programme outlined above in terms of the concept of 'combinatorial evolution' used by Brian Arthur (2010) in his book *The Nature of Technology*. His starting point, mainly in terms of 'hard' technology, is that the big complex systems sit at the top of a hierarchy of systems – think of aeroplanes, then engines and wings, then turbo blades and so on – much more complicated than that of course. His key argument is, then, that evolutions – advances – mainly take place at lower levels in the hierarchy, and then through new combinations of those advances. In our case, our top-level system of interest is, say, a city. A retail system is at the next level down in the hierarchy. Arthur's argument can be applied not just to the systems themselves – though it can, think of technologies impacting on cities and retailing – but also on the *science* of these systems, and modelling is an element of that science. What we have demonstrated in this book is that understanding of the dynamical systems through extended Lotka-Volterra equations, increased computing power and innovative visualisation offers a lower-level set of technologies that can then be applied at higher levels. In particular, the planning system itself can be seen as a high-level system, and we have explored the contributions of dynamic modelling – from lower down the hierarchy – to increase effectiveness at the higher levels.

So this helps us to interpret what we have achieved, but it also provides a framework within which we can seek further advances, some of which we have indicated both throughout the book and in this last chapter. The increasing power of the modelling 'technology', and all the associated technologies, presage an exciting future for this field.

References

Arthur, B. (2010) *The Nature of Technology*, London: Allen Lane, The Penguin Press.
Birkin, M., Clarke, G. P., Clarke, M. and Wilson, A. G. (1996) *Intelligent GIS: Location Decisions and Strategic Planning*, Cambridge: Geo-Information International.
de Martinis, V., Pagliara F. and Wilson A. G. (2014) 'The evolution and planning of hierarchical transport networks', *Environment and Planning B: Planning and Design*, 41(2): 192–210.
Richardson, L. F. (1960) *Arms and Insecurity: A Mathematical Study of the Causes and Origins of War*, Pittsburgh, PA: Boxwood Press.
Roumpani, F. and Wilson, A. (2014) *Digital Planning: Ideas to Make it Happen*, Royal Institute of British Architects, Think Piece Series, available at: http://issuu.com/ribacomms/docs/riba_think_piece_series_-_digital_p?e=2663058/7886017 (accessed 21 May 2014).
Wilson, A. G. (2007) 'A generalised representation for a comprehensive urban and regional model', *Computers, Environment and Urban Systems*, 31(2): 148–61.

Index